One Hundred and One Poems
by Paul Verlaine

One Hundred and One Poems by

Paul Verlaine

A Bilingual Edition

Translated by Norman R. Shapiro

THE UNIVERSITY OF CHICAGO PRESS ❖ CHICAGO AND LONDON

NORMAN R. SHAPIRO is professor of Romance languages and literatures at Wesleyan University. Among his many translations are *Fifty Fables of La Fontaine* (1988) and *Fifty More Fables of La Fontaine* (1997); *The Fabulists French: Verse Fables of Nine Centuries* (1992), winner of the ALTA Distinguished Translation Award for 1993; *Four Farces by Georges Feydeau,* published by the University of Chicago Press in 1971 and nominated for the National Book Award in the translations category; and *Selected Poems from 'Les Fleurs du mal,'* published by the University of Chicago Press in 1998.

The University of Chicago Press, Chicago 60637
The University of Chicago Press, Ltd., London
© 1999 by The University of Chicago
All rights reserved. Published 1999
08 07 06 05 04 03 02 01 00 99   1 2 3 4 5
ISBN: 0-226-85344-6 (cloth)

Library of Congress Cataloging-in-Publication Data
Verlaine, Paul, 1844–1896.
   [Poems. English & French. Selections]
   One Hundred and one poems by Paul Verlaine : a bilingual edition /
translated by Norman R. Shapiro.
     p.   cm.
   Includes bibliographical references and index.
   ISBN 0-226-85344-6 (cloth : alk. paper)
   I. Shapiro, Norman R.   II. Title.   III. Title: 101 poems by Paul Verlaine
PQ2463.A275   1999
841'.8—dc21   98-29016
                                          CIP

For Sylvia and Allan Kliman,
for their encouragement, concern, and affection

Contents

from *Épigrammes* (1894)

from *Chair* (1896)

from *Invectives* (1896)

Illustrations

Preface

A good many years ago, as an undergraduate, I concocted a
paper on Paul Verlaine, one of my favorite poets then as now.
And rightly so. But good aesthetic judgment does not neces-
sarily make for good academic writing; and over the years I
have continued to feel a little guilty at having been graduated
from a prestigious institution of higher learning with a
senior essay that, my then professors' opinions to the con-
trary notwithstanding, strikes me as having reflected little
credit on me and not much more on Verlaine. To salve my
conscience after all this time, I would like to consider the
present volume as something of a belated expiatory offering
(in retrospect, and with the improved vision of hindsight)
both to myself and to him. Or at least to his memory.

   This is a collection of translations; English versions of
poems by one of France's, and western literature's, most
gifted and prolific poets. It is not a dissection, a literary study
purporting to analyze his verse according to the canons of
this or that critical "ism," traditional or modish. And it is
certainly not a detailed biography. Any good encyclopedia
article on Verlaine will acquaint the reader with the salient
facts of his tormented life and of his artistic role in the
development of French poetry. Which is not to say that his
biography is unimportant to an understanding of his work in
general and of specific works in particular. On the contrary.
Though we were assured, not many decades ago, that biogra-
phy is irrelevant to an aesthetic appreciation of "the poem
itself"—or, indeed, of any literary work—I never believed it.
And while the New Criticism fades with age to become,
today, with a trace of a smirk, "the *old* New Criticism," oth-

ers are coming out of the critical closet to admit that they
never really believed it either.

In Verlaine's case, while it is possible, even easy, to appre-
ciate *in vacuo* the medium of his verse—its varied forms, its
flexible rhythms, its lush musicality—it is quite another mat-
ter for his messages. Not to know the circumstances that sur-
rounded and gave birth to his poems is, in many cases, really
not to comprehend them, in the fullest etymological sense of
that verb. This is true even for his more "universal" but
often heavily allegorical poems of religious fervor, rather few
of which I include, preferring by far the more idiosyncratic
earlier and later works (many, if not most, of the latter, usu-
ally neglected, being translated here for the first time). I
think that the brief headnotes to each section of this volume,
as well as the notes to many of the individual translations,
will provide the reader with enough of that indispensable or
ancillary biographical background to meet this need, at least
in its essentials.[*]

❋ THESE TRANSLATIONS were written during the summer
and fall of 1997, but the inspiration for them goes back many
years. Indeed, many decades. I am happy to express my grat-
itude to Seymour O. Simches, who, the first to introduce me
to the wonders of Verlaine and his melodious genius, nur-
tured and channeled that inspiration—though, at the time,
surely neither he nor I suspected that this volume would be
the result. I am grateful to him, both for his past role and for
his many years of encouragement; and, likewise, to friend

---

[*]The French texts reproduced in this volume are taken from a 1968 printing of
Jacques Borel's substantially augmented 1962 revision (Paris: Gallimard, 1962) of
Yves-Gérard Le Dantec's definitive edition of Verlaine's *Œuvres poétiques complètes*,
in the series Bibliothèque de la Pléiade (Paris: Gallimard, 1948).

Willis Barnstone, for his much more recent role in reviving my inspiration with a suggestion, albeit offhandedly proffered, that Verlaine would be a worthy subject to follow on the heels of my recent Baudelaire collection.

With this volume, no less than with all my incursions into verse translation, the example of my late mother's poetic talents has continued to inspire as well. I think that, thanks to her, I learned to spout rhymes in iambs and trochees almost before I learned to speak prose.

My thanks to Wesleyan University for its support of my endeavors, including a grant from the Thomas and Catharine McMahon Fund, established through the generosity of the late Joseph McMahon; to Adams House, Harvard University, under the aegis of Robert and Jana Kiely, and Vicki Macy, for offering a generous hospitality that has made much of my past and recent work possible; to Steve Sylvester and the staff of the Imaging Studio Services of Widener Library; and to Morris Philipson and Randolph Petilos of the University of Chicago Press for their confidence and patience, as well as to Russell Harper for his editorial skills.

Again, as with my other volumes, a number of good friends have been especially helpful. To Lillian Bulwa, Carla Chrisfield, Rita Dempsey, and Caldwell Titcomb, my sincere appreciation for their varied contributions to this endeavor.

And to Evelyn Singer Simha, who, as so often in the past, has given, without stint, of her warm heart, sharp ear, and sound judgment, a very special "thank you."

—*Norman R. Shapiro*

Poèmes saturniens (1866)

*W*hether, as a youth of twenty-two, Verlaine truly felt himself to have been born under the malevolent sign of Saturn, foreboding, this early in his life, of the dual nature of his conflicted personality, or whether this was only the aesthetic, self-indulgent posturing of an adulator of Baudelaire and his "flowers of evil," the fact is, his *Poèmes saturniens* really have very little "saturnine" about them except for the volume's title and a brief self-conscious liminary poem. His first collection to see print (though it does not include all his earliest verse), it was brought out in 1866, ostensibly by well-known Paris publisher Alphonse Lemerre, but actually subsidized by the young poet himself, thanks to the generosity of a doting female cousin whose death, a few years later, was to affect him deeply.

The collection, comprising four groupings entitled *Melancholia, Eaux-fortes* (Etchings), *Paysages tristes* (Sad Landscapes), and *Caprices,* as well as a dozen miscellaneous poems, brought together products of Verlaine's early years as a frequenter of the salon of the Marquise de Ricard and other social venues, where he rubbed shoulders with prominent artistic figures of the day, the likes of Anatole France, Emmanuel Chabrier, inventor-poet and humorist Charles Cros, the cynical antibourgeois idealist Auguste de Villiers de l'Isle-Adam, and, especially, the then important poets Théodore de Banville, François Coppée, José-María de

Heredia, Leconte de Lisle, and Catulle Mendès, all of whom were to leave their mark.

While the predominant poetic taste and style of the period glorified the impassivity and pictorial impersonality of the so-called Parnassians, who took their name from the several successive volumes of *Le Parnasse contemporain,* and although Verlaine, eager to espouse that prevailing "art for art's sake" ethos, managed to follow it up to a point and for a time, he was quite unable to rein in his innately lyrical and self-revelatory genius for long. Be it in neatly crafted sonnets, a form inherited from the past and transmitted by the idolized Baudelaire, or be it in free-form, lushly sonorous vignettes of his own confection, Verlaine's *Poèmes saturniens* offer the emerging poet's synthesis of the cerebral and the visceral, the descriptively objective and the melancholically subjective, the aesthetically detached and the personally involved, and already show his great range of formal, visual, musical, and sentimental artistry.

❊

Mon Rêve familier

Je fais souvent ce rêve étrange et pénétrant
D'une femme inconnue, et que j'aime, et qui m'aime
Et qui n'est, chaque fois, ni tout à fait la même
Ni tout à fait une autre, et m'aime et me comprend.

Car elle me comprend, et mon cœur, transparent
Pour elle seule, hélas! cesse d'être un problème
Pour elle seule, et les moiteurs de mon front blême,
Elle seule les sait rafraîchir, en pleurant.

Est-elle brune, blonde ou rousse?—Je l'ignore.
Son nom? Je me souviens qu'il est doux et sonore
Comme ceux des aimés que la Vie exila.

Son regard est pareil au regard des statues,
Et, pour sa voix, lointaine, et calme, et grave, elle a
L'inflexion des voix chères qui se sont tues.

MELANCHOLIA, VI

My Familiar Dream

Often I dream this poignant fantasy,
Strange, of a woman never met, but who
Loves me, and whom I love, and who seems new
Each time and yet who seems the same; and she

Loves me, and understands the mystery
Clouding my heart, as no one else can do;
And who, alone, with tears fresh as the dew,
Soothes, cools my pale and fevered brow for me.

Her hair? Red, blond, or brown? I don't know which.
Nor do I know her name. But lush and rich
It is, like those of friends once loved, exiled

By Life. Her glance? A statue's glance. And for
Her voice, it sings—distant and mellow, mild—
The music of dear voices heard no more.

MELANCHOLIA, VI

Marine

L'Océan sonore
Palpite sous l'œil
De la lune en deuil
Et palpite encore,

Tandis qu'un éclair
Brutal et sinistre
Fend le ciel de bistre
D'un long zigzag clair,

Et que chaque lame
En bonds convulsifs
Le long des récifs
Va, vient, luit et clame,

Et qu'au firmament,
Où l'ouragan erre,
Rugit le tonnerre
Formidablement.

EAUX - FORTES , III

Seascape

The moon, in mourning, eyes
The moaning, churning sea,
Churning up endlessly
While, in the copper skies,

A heaven-splitting crash—
Like clashing stroke of doom—
Streaks, zigzags through the gloom
Its long, bright lightning flash;

On, on the surf swells, rolls,
Breaks with convulsive bounds—
Comes, goes—glistens, resounds
Against the rocky shoals;

On, on, rumbling asunder,
The very firmament,
Everywhere tempest-rent,
Roars with its mighty thunder.

EAUX-FORTES, III

Effet de nuit

La nuit. La pluie. Un ciel blafard que déchiquette
De flèches et de tours à jour la silhouette
D'une ville gothique éteinte au lointain gris.
La plaine. Un gibet plein de pendus rabougris
Secoués par le bec avide des corneilles
Et dansant dans l'air noir des gigues nonpareilles,
Tandis que leurs pieds sont la pâture des loups.
Quelques buissons d'épine épars, et quelques houx
Dressant l'horreur de leur feuillage à droite, à gauche,
Sur le fuligineux fouillis d'un fond d'ébauche.
Et puis, autour de trois livides prisonniers
Qui vont pieds nus, un gros de hauts pertuisaniers
En marche, et leurs fers droits, comme des fers de herse,
Luisent à contre-sens des lances de l'averse.

EAUX-FORTES, IV

Night Scene

Night. Rain. Spires, empty-windowed turrets, jutting;
A distant, lifeless Gothic city, cutting
Sharp silhouettes against a sallow sky.
The plain. A gibbet, corpses hanging high,
Withered and wizened, swinging, raven-pecked,
Dancing weird nighttime jigs, while wolves collect,
Ravenous, foraging upon their feet.
Against a background, outlined, incomplete—
Bramble-twined chaos, murky mass—left, right,
A bush, a briar, pushing its ghostly height.
And there, marching three prisoners—ashen faces,
Barefoot—a squad of halberdiers: their maces,
Stiff as portcullis spikes, rise from the plain,
Glistening athwart the javelins of the rain.

EAUX-FORTES, IV

Soleils couchants

Une aube affaiblie
Verse par les champs
La mélancolie
Des soleils couchants.
La mélancolie
Berce de doux chants
Mon cœur qui s'oublie
Aux soleils couchants.
Et d'étranges rêves,
Comme des soleils
Couchants sur les grèves,
Fantômes vermeils,
Défilent sans trêves,
Défilent, pareils
À des grands soleils
Couchants sur les grèves.

PAYSAGES TRISTES, I

Sunsets

Dim-dawning glow
Of breaking morn
Rains here below
The hope forlorn
And wistful woe
Of sunsets born.
Their wistful woe
Lulls, cradles me,
And fills my soul
With fantasy:
Dream-sunsets—droll,
Strange—reverie
Of trolls a-stroll
Unceasingly,
On shore and shoal:
Sunsets a-stroll
Astride the sea.

PAYSAGES TRISTES , I

Crépuscule du soir mystique

Le Souvenir avec le Crépuscule
Rougeoie et tremble à l'ardent horizon
De l'Espérance en flamme qui recule
Et s'agrandit ainsi qu'une cloison
Mystérieuse où mainte floraison
—Dahlia, lys, tulipe et renoncule—
S'élance autour d'un treillis, et circule
Parmi la maladive exhalaison
De parfums lourds et chauds, dont le poison
—Dahlia, lys, tulipe et renoncule—
Noyant mes sens, mon âme et ma raison,
Mêle dans une immense pâmoison
Le Souvenir avec le Crépuscule.

PAYSAGES TRISTES, II

Mystical Evening Twilight

Memory, with the Twilight's dusky light,
Reddening, trembles on the burning sky's
Hope-filled horizon: flames that, in their height,
Glimmering backward, forward, seem to rise
Like some mysterious wall, where, trellis-wise,
Many a flower lies in the gathering night
—Buttercup, dahlia, tulip, lily white—
Spread, basking in their heavy-perfumed sighs,
Hot, torpid-breathed, whose poisons mesmerize
—Buttercup, dahlia, tulip, lily white—
And drown my mind, my soul, my ears, my eyes
In one consuming swoon, where, listless, lies
Memory, with the Twilight's dusky light.

PAYSAGES TRISTES, II

Promenade sentimentale

Le couchant dardait ses rayons suprêmes
Et le vent berçait les nénuphars blêmes;
Les grands nénuphars entre les roseaux
Tristement luisaient sur les calmes eaux.
Moi j'errais tout seul, promenant ma plaie
Au long de l'étang, parmi la saulaie
Où la brume vague évoquait un grand
Fantôme laiteux se désespérant
Et pleurant avec la voix des sarcelles
Qui se rappelaient en battant des ailes
Parmi la saulaie où j'errais tout seul
Promenant ma plaie; et l'épais linceul
Des ténèbres vint noyer les suprêmes
Rayons du couchant dans ces ondes blêmes
Et les nénuphars, parmi les roseaux,
Les grands nénuphars sur les calmes eaux.

PAYSAGES TRISTES, III

Sentimental Stroll

The sunset darted low its splendorous rays;
The wind cradled and swayed the pallid haze
Of waterlilies in the reeds beyond,
Glistening, sad and tranquil, on the pond.
And I, alone, roamed with my agonies,
Wandered the shore among the willow trees,
Where milk-white mist hung vaguely in the air,
Phantom-like form, bewailing its despair
And weeping with the voice of seabirds' sputter,
Calling each other nestward, wings aflutter
Among the willow trees, where I, alone,
Roamed with my agonies; the shadows, sewn
Into a shroud, drowned deep the sunset's rays,
Splendorous, sinking in the billows' haze;
And waterlilies in the reeds beyond...
Great lilies, lying tranquil, on the pond.

PAYSAGES TRISTES, III

Chanson d'automne

Les sanglots longs
Des violons
   De l'automne
Blessent mon cœur
D'une langueur
   Monotone.

Tout suffocant
Et blême, quand
   Sonne l'heure,
Je me souviens
Des jours anciens
   Et je pleure;

Et je m'en vais
Au vent mauvais
   Qui m'emporte
Deçà, delà,
Pareil à la
   Feuille morte.

PAYSAGES TRISTES, V

Autumn Song

The autumn's throbbing
Strings moan, sobbing,
    Drone their dole;
Long-drawn and low,
Each tremolo
    Sears my soul.

When tolls the hour
I think of our
    Days gone by;
Pallid as death
I gasp for breath,
    And I cry.

And like a dead
Leaf, buffeted,
    Tempest-tossed,
I ride the air—
Now here, now there—
    Aimless, lost…

PAYSAGES TRISTES, V

L'Heure du berger

La lune est rouge au brumeux horizon;
Dans un brouillard qui danse la prairie
S'endort fumeuse, et la grenouille crie
Par les joncs verts où circule un frisson;

Les fleurs des eaux referment leurs corolles;
Des peupliers profilent aux lointains,
Droits et serrés, leurs spectres incertains;
Vers les buissons errent les lucioles;

Les chats-huants s'éveillent, et sans bruit
Rament l'air noir avec leurs ailes lourdes,
Et le zénith s'emplit de lueurs sourdes.
Blanche, Vénus émerge, et c'est la Nuit.

PAYSAGES TRISTES, VI

The Shepherd's Hour

The rising moon shines reddish through the mist;
Amid the smoke-like, quivering haze, the field
Drops off to sleep; the frog croaks, squawks, concealed
Among the shivering reeds, green, zephyr-kissed.

The water-flowers close up their petals, while
Fireflies go flitting over bush and briar;
Distant, dim poplar-ghosts stretch higher and higher
Their slender silhouettes in single file.

The hoot-owls, silent, wake and take their flight,
Plowing the black air with their weighty wings;
The heavens fill with soundless glitterings.
White, Venus sallies forth, and it is night.

PAYSAGES TRISTES, VI

Femme et chatte

Elle jouait avec sa chatte,
Et c'était merveille de voir
La main blanche et la blanche patte
S'ébattre dans l'ombre du soir.

Elle cachait—la scélérate!—
Sous ses mitaines de fil noir
Ses meurtriers ongles d'agate,
Coupants et clairs comme un rasoir.

L'autre aussi faisait la sucrée
Et rentrait sa griffe acérée,
Mais le diable n'y perdait rien…

Et dans le boudoir où, sonore,
Tintait son rire aérien,
Brillaient quatre points de phosphore.

CAPRICES, I

Woman and Cat

It was a joy to watch as she
Played with her cat: white hand, paw white
As well. What a delight to see
Both frolic in the shadowed night.

She hid her nails—perfidiously!—
Within black mittens, out of sight,
Fine agate nails, bright as could be,
Like razors, sharp, and deadly, quite.

The kitten, playing just as sweet,
Drew in her devil-claws, discreet,
But profited no less, in essence:

Madame's boudoir… Her laughter, blowing
Light on the air, a-peal. And, glowing,
Gleaming, four orbs of phosphorescence.

CAPRICES, I

Un Dahlia

Courtisane au sein dur, à l'œil opaque et brun
S'ouvrant avec lenteur comme celui d'un bœuf,
Ton grand torse reluit ainsi qu'un marbre neuf.

Fleur grasse et riche, autour de toi ne flotte aucun
Arome, et la beauté sereine de ton corps
Déroule, mate, ses impeccables accords.

Tu ne sens même pas la chair, ce goût qu'au moins
Exhalent celles-là qui vont fanant les foins,
Et tu trônes, Idole insensible à l'encens.

—Ainsi le Dahlia, roi vêtu de splendeur,
Élève sans orgueil sa tête sans odeur,
Irritant au milieu des jasmins agaçants!

A Dahlia

Hard-bosomed courtesan, magnificent
Marble-glossed figure; eye opaque, of solid
Brown, opening like a bull's, languid and stolid.

Flower ornate and richly plump; no scent
Wafts round you, and your body's graceful ease
Rolls free—then mutes—its flawless harmonies.

Yours is not even flesh's scent, that those
Hay-tossing belles exude; rather, you pose,
Idol unmoved by incense burned before you.

—Such is the Dahlia, king nobly costumed:
You hold your head high, modest, unperfumed,
Irksome, among the jasmines, who abhor you!

Nevermore

Allons, mon pauvre cœur, allons, *mon vieux complice,*
Redresse et peins à neuf tous tes arcs triomphaux;
Brûle un encens ranci sur tes autels d'or faux;
Sème de fleurs les bords béants du précipice;
Allons, mon pauvre cœur, allons, *mon vieux complice!*

Pousse à Dieu ton cantique, ô chantre rajeuni;
Entonne, orgue enroué, des *Te Deum* splendides;
Vieillard prématuré, mets du fard sur tes rides;
Couvre-toi de tapis mordorés, mur jauni;
Pousse à Dieu ton cantique, ô chantre rajeuni.

Sonnez, grelots; sonnez, clochettes; sonnez, cloches!
Car mon rêve impossible a pris corps, et je l'ai
Entre mes bras pressé: le Bonheur, cet ailé
Voyageur qui de l'Homme évite les approches,
—Sonnez, grelots; sonnez, clochettes; sonnez, cloches!

Le Bonheur a marché côte à côte avec moi;
Mais la FATALITÉ ne connaît point de trêve:
Le ver est dans le fruit, le réveil dans le rêve,
Et le remords est dans l'amour: telle est la loi.
—Le Bonheur a marché côte à côte avec moi.

Nevermore

Come, my poor heart, come, *old friend true and tried,*
Repaint your triumph's arches, raised anew;
Smoke tinsel altars with stale incense; strew
Flowers before the chasm, gaping wide;
Come, my poor heart, come, *old friend true and tried.*

Cantor revivified, sing God your hymn;
Hoarse organ-pipes, intone *Te Deums* proud;
Make up your aging face, youth wrinkle-browed;
Bedeck yourself in gold, wall yellow-dim;
Cantor revivified, sing God your hymn.

Ring, bells; peal, chimes; peal, ring, bells large and small!
My hopeless dream takes shape: for Happiness—
Here, now—lies clutched, embraced in my caress;
Winged Voyager, who shuns Man's every call;
—Ring, bells; peal, chimes; peal, ring, bells large and small!

Happiness once walked side by side with me;
But DOOM knows no reprieve, there's no mistaking:
The worm is in the fruit; in dreaming, waking;
In loving, mourning. And so must it be.
—Happiness once walked side by side with me.

Fêtes galantes (1869)

*A*lthough they created little critical stir upon publication, the twenty-two generally brief poems of *Fêtes galantes* —only three are over twenty lines long, and most hover between twelve and twenty—are "pure Verlaine." That is, it is their delicacy of touch, their metrical fluidity within formal constraints, and their evocative musicality of tone that one thinks of, rather than their superficially Parnassian descriptiveness, when one would typify his art. These "gallant revels" were inspired, clearly, by the dreamlike scenes and traditional *commedia dell'arte* characters borrowed from the canvases of the painter Watteau. It is no mere coincidence that Verlaine was a frequent visitor to the Salle Lacaze, in the Louvre, where an exhibition of Watteau, Lancret, the equally elegant Fragonard, and other eighteenth-century French masters had opened in 1867, two years before publication of this collection.

Fêtes galantes appeared in 1869, published, like the *Poèmes saturniens,* by Lemerre. It was actually Verlaine's third collection if one counts a clandestine volume, *Les Amies, scènes d'amour sapphique,* pornographic by the period's standards, brought out in Brussels in December of 1867 under the fanciful and transparent pseudonym Pablo-María de Herlagnèz (or Herlañes) by Baudelaire's erstwhile publisher Poulet-Malassis. Six months later the work was seized and destroyed by the French government, and the publisher, no stranger to moral controversy, was obliged to pay a fine.

In striking contrast to the carnality of *Les Amies*, whose sonnets, somewhat revised, would appear later in the collection *Parallèlement*, the vaporous, moonlit atmosphere of the scenarios depicted in the lapidary *Fêtes galantes* is only innocently erotic, and almost chastely suggestive in its mannered gaiety and *précieux* melancholy, shaded in the most delicate of mezzotints.

※

Clair de lune

Votre âme est un paysage choisi
Que vont charmant masques et bergamasques
Jouant du luth et dansant et quasi
Tristes sous leurs déguisements fantasques.

Tout en chantant sur le mode mineur
L'amour vainqueur et la vie opportune,
Ils n'ont pas l'air de croire à leur bonheur
Et leur chanson se mêle au clair de lune,

Au calme clair de lune triste et beau,
Qui fait rêver les oiseaux dans les arbres
Et sangloter d'extase les jets d'eau,
Les grands jets d'eau sveltes parmi les marbres.

Moonlight

Your soul is like a landscape fantasy,
Where masks and Bergamasks, in charming wise,
Strum lutes and dance, just a bit sad to be
Hidden beneath their fanciful disguise.

Singing in minor mode of life's largesse
And all-victorious love, they yet seem quite
Reluctant to believe their happiness,
And their song mingles with the pale moonlight,

The calm, pale moonlight, whose sad beauty, beaming,
Sets the birds softly dreaming in the trees,
And makes the marbled fountains, gushing, streaming—
Slender jet-fountains—sob their ecstasies.

Pantomime

Pierrot, qui n'a rien d'un Clitandre,
Vide un flacon sans plus attendre,
Et, pratique, entame un pâté.

Cassandre, au fond de l'avenue,
Verse une larme méconnue
Sur son neveu déshérité.

Ce faquin d'Arlequin combine
L'enlèvement de Colombine
Et pirouette quatre fois.

Colombine rêve, surprise
De sentir un cœur dans la brise
Et d'entendre en son cœur des voix.

Pantomime

Pierrot—no swain Clitander, he—
Swills from a flagon gluttonously,
Cuts into a pâté. (Why wait?)

Off in the distance, old compeer
Cassander sheds a furtive tear
Over his disowned nephew's fate.

Harlequin, roguish varlet, yearns
To kidnap Colombine, then turns
Four pirouettes with flawless art.

Colombine dreams, stands musing there,
Awed to hear heartbeats in the air
And voices whispering in her heart.

Sur l'herbe

L'abbé divague.—Et toi, marquis,
Tu mets de travers ta perruque.
—Ce vieux vin de Chypre est exquis
Moins, Camargo, que votre nuque.

—Ma flamme…—Do, mi, sol, la, si.
L'abbé, ta noirceur se dévoile!
—Que je meure, Mesdames, si
Je ne vous décroche une étoile!

—Je voudrais être petit chien!
—Embrassons nos bergères l'une
Après l'autre.—Messieurs, eh bien?
—Do, mi, sol.—Hé! bonsoir, la Lune!

On the Grass

"Marquis, your wig is crooked." "Mine?"
"Your shoulders, Camargo… Exquisite…"
Drones the *abbé*… "More than this fine
Old wine, my dear… From Cyprus, is it?…

"My love…" "Do, mi, sol, la, si, do…"
"My heart…" "Is full of guile, *abbé!*"
"Upon my soul, *mesdames*, I'll go
Pluck you all stars…" "Sol, fa, mi, re…"

"Let's kiss, each one, our shepherdesses…"
"Would I were but a puppy…" "Oh?…"
"Ah so, *messieurs?* And those caresses?…"
"Good evening, Moon!…" "Fa, mi, re, do…"

L'Allée

Fardée et peinte comme au temps des bergeries,
Frêle parmi les nœuds énormes de rubans,
Elle passe, sous les ramures assombries,
Dans l'allée où verdit la mousse des vieux bancs,
Avec mille façons et mille afféteries
Qu'on garde d'ordinaire aux perruches chéries.
Sa longue robe à queue est bleue, et l'éventail
Qu'elle froisse en ses doigts fluets aux larges bagues
S'égaie en des sujets érotiques, si vagues
Qu'elle sourit, tout en rêvant, à maint détail.
—Blonde en somme. Le nez mignon avec la bouche
Incarnadine, grasse et divine d'orgueil
Inconscient.—D'ailleurs, plus fine que la mouche
Qui ravive l'éclat un peu niais de l'œil.

The Lane

Face painted, powdered, as in olden days'
Pastoral revelries; frail in her masses
Of ribbons, giant bows, beneath the maze
Of shaded boughs that line the lane; she passes
Among old green-mossed benches, and displays
Her myriad posturings and mannered ways
That one might lavish most on pet cuckoos.
Her trailing gown is blue; her long ringed fingers
Rumple a fan as, musing, her smile lingers
Over its vaguely bawdy curlicues.
Blonde, with a pert nose; coral lips, full, proud—
Unwitting pride! A beauty spot enhances
Those lips divine, contriving to uncloud
The slightly daft flamboyance of her glances.

À la promenade

Le ciel si pâle et les arbres si grêles
Semblent sourire à nos costumes clairs
Qui vont flottant légers, avec des airs
De nonchalance et des mouvements d'ailes.

Et le vent doux ride l'humble bassin,
Et la lueur du soleil qu'atténue
L'ombre des bas tilleuls de l'avenue
Nous parvient bleue et mourante à dessein.

Trompeurs exquis et coquettes charmantes,
Cœurs tendres, mais affranchis du serment,
Nous devisons délicieusement,
Et les amants lutinent les amantes,

De qui la main imperceptible sait
Parfois donner un soufflet, qu'on échange
Contre un baiser sur l'extrême phalange
Du petit doigt, et comme la chose est

Immensément excessive et farouche,
On est puni par un regard très sec,
Lequel contraste, au demeurant, avec
La moue assez clémente de la bouche.

Strolling

The sky so pale, the trees so spindly, bare,
Seem to be smiling at our costumes: bright,
Wind-blown and nonchalant, as if they might
Be wings aflutter, floating on the air.

The pool's face puckers in the gentle breeze,
The glimmering sun casts deep blue shadows through
The linden trees that line the avenue;
Shades to abet and serve our coquetries.

Men—dashing rakes—and ladies—sly coquettes—
Dear hearts, unbound by oaths and fancy-free,
We prattle each to each, beguilingly;
And lovers twit and taunt their mignonettes,

Whose hands, at times, are quick to trade a cuff—
Sharp, unobserved—against those wandering lips
That plant a kiss on dainty fingertips:
A scurvy deed and dastardly enough

To earn the cad the bitterest glance; no doubt,
Punishment most severe, but, by the way,
One that their lovely mouths belie, as they
Purse in a coy and all-forgiving pout.

Les Ingénus

Les hauts talons luttaient avec les longues jupes,
En sorte que, selon le terrain et le vent,
Parfois luisaient des bas de jambes, trop souvent
Interceptés!—et nous aimions ce jeu de dupes.

Parfois aussi le dard d'un insecte jaloux
Inquiétait le col des belles sous les branches,
Et c'étaient des éclairs soudains de nuques blanches,
Et ce régal comblait nos jeunes yeux de fous.

Le soir tombait, un soir équivoque d'automne:
Les belles, se pendant rêveuses à nos bras,
Dirent alors des mots si spécieux, tout bas,
Que notre âme, depuis ce temps, tremble et s'étonne.

Innocents We

Their long skirts and high heels battled away:
Depending on the ground's and breezes' whim,
At times some stocking shone, low on the limb—
Too soon concealed!—tickling our naïveté.

At times, as well, an envious bug would bite
Our lovelies' necks beneath the boughs, and we
Would glimpse a flash—white flesh, ah! ecstasy!—
And glut our mad young eyes on sheer delight.

Evening would fall, the autumn day would draw
To its uncertain close: our belles would cling
Dreamingly to us, cooing, whispering
Lies that still set our souls trembling with awe.

Cortège

Un singe en veste de brocart
Trotte et gambade devant elle
Qui froisse un mouchoir de dentelle
Dans sa main gantée avec art,

Tandis qu'un négrillon tout rouge
Maintient à tour de bras les pans
De sa lourde robe en suspens,
Attentif à tout pli qui bouge;

Le singe ne perd pas des yeux
La gorge blanche de la dame,
Opulent trésor que réclame
Le torse nu de l'un des dieux;

Le négrillon parfois soulève
Plus haut qu'il ne faut, l'aigrefin,
Son fardeau somptueux, afin
De voir ce dont la nuit il rêve;

Elle va par les escaliers,
Et ne paraît pas davantage
Sensible à l'insolent suffrage
De ses animaux familiers.

Cortège

An ape, in brocade jacket dressed,
Gambols before her, trots apace,
As she crumples a kerchief's lace
In hand gloved of the loveliest;

Behind, a pygmy, ruddy-hued,
Holds her train off the ground, and finds
The armfuls burdensome, yet minds
Each fold with much solicitude;

The ape surveys with eager eye
Her bosom, pale and splendor-fraught,
Luxuriant treasure much besought
By naked-breasted god on high;

The pygmy—slyboots!—raises slightly
Higher, from time to time, than he
Ought do, his sumptuous load, to see
The pleasure that he dreams of nightly;

Upstairs and down she goes, betraying
Never the merest notion of
The lustful looks—below, above—
Brash tribute that her pets are paying.

Les Coquillages

Chaque coquillage incrusté
Dans la grotte où nous nous aimâmes
A sa particularité.

L'un a la pourpre de nos âmes
Dérobée au sang de nos cœurs
Quand je brûle et que tu t'enflammes;

Cet autre affecte tes langueurs
Et tes pâleurs alors que, lasse,
Tu m'en veux de mes yeux moqueurs;

Celui-ci contrefait la grâce
De ton oreille, et celui-là
Ta nuque rose, courte et grasse;

Mais un, entre autres, me troubla.

Seashells

Each seashell in the walls where we
Made love—our grotto rendezvous—
Has its own special property.

One has our souls' deep crimson hue
Snatched from our hearts' blood when I flare
And flame with passion, as do you;

This one affects that look you wear—
Languid and pale—when, listless, spent,
You scold me for my mocking air;

This one would sport the innocent
Curve of your ear; that one, like bud
Of rose, your neck's: pink, corpulent;

But one there was that fired my blood.

Fantoches

Scaramouche et Pulcinella
Qu'un mauvais dessein rassembla
Gesticulent, noirs sur la lune.

Cependant l'excellent docteur
Bolonais cueille avec lenteur
Des simples parmi l'herbe brune.

Lors sa fille, piquant minois,
Sous la charmille, en tapinois,
Se glisse, demi-nue, en quête

De son beau pirate espagnol,
Dont un langoureux rossignol
Clame la détresse à tue-tête.

Puppets

Polichinelle and his colleague
Sly Scaramouche, in some intrigue,
Dark-silhouetted, rave and rant.

Meanwhile, old papa Pantaloon,
Picking his herbs against the moon,
Goes lumbering from plant to plant.

His daughter—dainty morsel, she—
Half-dressed, goes slipping stealthily
Under the arbor boughs, in quest

Of her stout Spanish buccaneer,
Whose parrot squawks, for all to hear,
The longings of a heart distressed.

En bateau

L'étoile du berger tremblote
Dans l'eau plus noire et le pilote
Cherche un briquet dans sa culotte.

C'est l'instant, Messieurs, ou jamais,
D'être audacieux, et je mets
Mes deux mains partout désormais!

Le chevalier Atys, qui gratte
Sa guitare, à Chloris l'ingrate
Lance une œillade scélérate.

L'abbé confesse bas Églé,
Et ce vicomte déréglé
Des champs donne à son cœur la clé.

Cependant la lune se lève
Et l'esquif en sa course brève
File gaîment sur l'eau qui rêve.

Sailing

The evening star flickers and glints
On darkling pool; the helmsman squints,
Searching his trousers for his flints.

Now is the time, Messieurs, or never.
Dare to be bold—like me—and clever:
My hands roam where they will, whenever!

Atys, our noble chevalier,
Strumming a tune, plucking away,
Leers at Chloris, whose eyes say "nay!"

The priest hears Sire Églé's confession,
Who, whispering many an indiscretion,
Sets his heart on his next transgression.

Meanwhile, up comes the moon; the bark
Gaily sails round the little park
Over the water, dreaming, dark.

Le Faune

Un vieux faune de terre cuite
Rit au centre des boulingrins,
Présageant sans doute une suite
Mauvaise à ces instants sereins

Qui m'ont conduit et t'ont conduite,
—Mélancoliques pèlerins,—
Jusqu'à cette heure dont la fuite
Tournoie au son des tambourins.

The Faun

An ancient terra cotta faun
Laughs on the green: sign, probably,
That something will rain woe upon
These moments of serenity

That led us here, and led us on,
You, me—nostalgic pilgrims, we—
To this one hour, now spun and gone
Midst tambourines' cacophony.

Mandoline

Les donneurs de sérénades
Et les belles écouteuses
Échangent des propos fades
Sous les ramures chanteuses.

C'est Tircis et c'est Aminte,
Et c'est l'éternel Clitandre,
Et c'est Damis qui pour mainte
Cruelle fait maint vers tendre.

Leurs courtes vestes de soie,
Leurs longues robes à queues,
Leur élégance, leur joie
Et leurs molles ombres bleues

Tourbillonnent dans l'extase
D'une lune rose et grise,
Et la mandoline jase
Parmi les frissons de brise.

Mandolin

There, beneath the echoing trees,
Renderers of serenades
Proffer their banalities
To their fair, attentive maids.

Tircis and Aminta too,
And Clitander, lost in time,
And the poet Damis, who
Plies cruel loves with endless rhyme.

Joyousness and elegance,
Fine long robes, silk waistcoats, and
Muted shadows join the dance
In a whirling saraband,

Blissful to be basking in
Pink-gray glories of the moon,
As, meanwhile, the mandolin
Twangs the breezes with its tune.

À Clymène

Mystiques barcarolles,
Romances sans paroles,
Chère, puisque tes yeux,
        Couleur des cieux,

Puisque ta voix, étrange
Vision qui dérange
Et trouble l'horizon
        De ma raison,

Puisque l'arome insigne
De ta pâleur de cygne,
Et puisque la candeur
        De ton odeur,

Ah! puisque tout ton être,
Musique qui pénètre,
Nimbes d'anges défunts,
        Tons et parfums,

A, sur d'almes cadences,
En ces correspondances
Induit mon cœur subtil,
        Ainsi soit-il!

For Clymène

Songs of the gondolier,
Vague, wordless airs; my dear,
Since your eyes, heaven-blue;
    Since your voice too,

Strange vision that upsets
The distant silhouettes
Lined up against the sky
    Of my mind's eye;

Since your skin's fragrance, bright
As the swan's brilliant white;
And since the pale pastel
    Of your sweet smell;

Ah! since your being entire—
Heavenly angel-choir
Haloed in death, perfumes,
    And sounds—subsumes

With cadence colorless
In its harmoniousness
My tenuous heart, amen!
    So be it then!

Colombine

Léandre le sot,
Pierrot qui d'un saut
        De puce
Franchit le buisson,
Cassandre sous son
        Capuce,

Arlequin aussi,
Cet aigrefin si
        Fantasque
Aux costumes fous,
Ses yeux luisants sous
        Son masque,

—Do, mi, sol, mi, fa,—
Tout ce monde va,
        Rit, chante
Et danse devant
Une belle enfant
        Méchante

Dont les yeux pervers
Comme les yeux verts
        Des chattes
Gardent ses appas
Et disent: "À bas
        Les pattes!"

Colombine

The dimwitted Leander,
The hood-headed Cassander,
       The spry
Pierrot, who, like a flea,
Springs, leaps the greenery;
       The sly

Harlequin too—that oh
So cunning domino,
       Whose eyes
Shine through that mask that is
So odd a part of his
       Disguise.

All of them "ooh" and "ah",
Giggle their fa-la-la,
       Laugh, sing,
Dance, utterly beguiled
By damsel fair. The child,
       Cruel thing,

Flashes her cat-eyes, green,
With callous looks that mean
       A scoff,
A sneer, and that, though they
Tempt and seduce, still say:
       "Hands off!"

—Eux ils vont toujours!
Fatidique cours
      Des astres,
Oh! dis-moi vers quels
Mornes ou cruels
      Désastres

L'implacable enfant,
Preste et relevant
      Ses jupes,
La rose au chapeau,
Conduit son troupeau
      De dupes?

Yet they press on! What force
Can halt the planets' course!
      Ah yes,
Tell me, oh, tell me, please,
Toward what calamity's
      Distress

(Rose in her bonnet, pert,
Taunting, with upheld skirt,
      Her troops)
The heartless wench will lure
Her *légion d'amour*
      Of dupes?

L'*Amour par terre*

Le vent de l'autre nuit a jeté bas l'Amour
Qui, dans le coin le plus mystérieux du parc,
Souriait en bandant malignement son arc,
Et dont l'aspect nous fit tant songer tout un jour!

Le vent de l'autre nuit l'a jeté bas! Le marbre
Au souffle du matin tournoie, épars. C'est triste
De voir le piédestal, où le nom de l'artiste
Se lit péniblement parmi l'ombre d'un arbre,

Oh! c'est triste de voir debout le piédestal
Tout seul! Et des pensers mélancoliques vont
Et viennent dans mon rêve où le chagrin profond
Évoque un avenir solitaire et fatal.

Oh! c'est triste!—Et toi-même, est-ce pas? es touchée
D'un si dolent tableau, bien que ton œil frivole
S'amuse au papillon de pourpre et d'or qui vole
Au-dessus des débris dont l'allée est jonchée.

Love Cast Down

The wind, one night, laid Cupid's statue low,
Which, in the park's most secret nook had stood;
Whose look, daylong, had charmed us, as we would
Muse on his sly smile and his tight-drawn bow.

The wind, one night, laid Cupid low. Ah me!
How bare his pedestal! The sculptor's name
Dims in the shadows and, the more the shame,
Dawn's breath whirls, swirls and scatters Love's debris.

How sad it is to see, standing there still,
That pedestal, alone, calling to mind
Dreams of a future of the drearest kind,
Waiting in solitude for death's dark chill.

How sad!—And you? Touched no less by the pains
Of such a sight, although your frivolous eye
Fancies the gold and purple butterfly
Flitting above Love's bower-blown remains.

En sourdine

Calmes dans le demi-jour
Que les branches hautes font,
Pénétrons bien notre amour
De ce silence profond.

Fondons nos âmes, nos cœurs
Et nos sens extasiés,
Parmi les vagues langueurs
Des pins et des arbousiers.

Ferme tes yeux à demi,
Croise tes bras sur ton sein,
Et de ton cœur endormi
Chasse à jamais tout dessein.

Laissons-nous persuader
Au souffle berceur et doux
Qui vient à tes pieds rider
Les ondes de gazon roux.

Et quand, solennel, le soir
Des chênes noirs tombera,
Voix de notre désespoir,
Le rossignol chantera.

In Muted Tone

Gently, let us steep our love
In the silence deep, as thus,
Branches arching high above
Twine their shadows over us.

Let us blend our souls as one,
Hearts' and senses' ecstasies,
Evergreen, in unison
With the pines' vague lethargies.

Dim your eyes and, heart at rest,
Freed from all futile endeavor,
Arms crossed on your slumbering breast,
Banish vain desire forever.

Let us yield then, you and I,
To the waftings, calm and sweet,
As their breeze-blown lullaby
Sways the gold grass at your feet.

And, when night begins to fall
From the black oaks, darkening,
In the nightingale's soft call
Our despair will, solemn, sing.

Colloque sentimental

Dans le vieux parc solitaire et glacé,
Deux formes ont tout à l'heure passé.

Leurs yeux sont morts et leurs lèvres sont molles,
Et l'on entend à peine leurs paroles.

Dans le vieux parc solitaire et glacé,
Deux spectres ont évoqué le passé.

—Te souvient-il de notre extase ancienne?
—Pourquoi voulez-vous donc qu'il m'en souvienne?

—Ton cœur bat-il toujours à mon seul nom?
Toujours vois-tu mon âme en rêve?—Non.

—Ah! les beaux jours de bonheur indicible
Où nous joignions nos bouches!—C'est possible.

—Qu'il était bleu, le ciel, et grand, l'espoir!
—L'espoir a fui, vaincu, vers le ciel noir.

Tels ils marchaient dans les avoines folles,
Et la nuit seule entendit leurs paroles.

Lovers' Chat

In the drear park, beneath a chill, bleak sky,
Two shapes, two silhouettes come passing by.

Lifeless their eyes, formless their lips; and they
Speak low, and muffled are the words they say.

In the drear park, beneath a chill, bleak sky,
Two phantom figures talk of days gone by.

"Do you remember how our souls would ache
With bliss?" "Why ask? What difference does it make?"

"Do I still haunt your dreams, like long ago?
Does my mere name still make your heart pound?" "No."

"Oh, for those wondrous days, the ecstasy,
Kiss upon kiss, pressed lips to lips!" "Maybe."

"How high our hopes, how blue the sky, outspread!"
"Dark now the sky, and, humbled, hope has fled!"

Treading the weeds, they talked the time away,
And night alone heard what they had to say.

La Bonne Chanson (1870)

Shortly before the publication of *Fêtes galantes*, Verlaine, continuing his worldly and artistic frequentations, had become a habitué of the prominent salon of the aristocratic social butterfly Nina de Villard, lover of Villiers de l'Isle-Adam, among others, and had come to know the musician Charles de Sivry. He and the latter soon became fast friends, and it was Sivry who introduced him to his half sister Mathilde Mauté, prim sixteen-year-old of a conventional bourgeois family (despite a fanciful "de Fleurville" tacked onto the surname).

Perhaps to defuse the urgings toward marriage and stability, proddings of his mother and other relatives concerned about Verlaine's already scandalous bouts with alcohol; perhaps to convince himself of a heterosexuality that a deep affection for Lucien Viotti, a colleague at the Lycée Bonaparte, had called into question; or perhaps, even, in complete sincerity (at least for the moment), the poet impulsively asked for Mathilde's hand in marriage. Rather to his surprise, his proposal was accepted, though not without hesitation on the part of the family, and the marriage took place in June of 1870.

The Mautés' misgivings were soon to prove only too well founded.

The poems of *La Bonne Chanson,* twenty-one in all, are the idealized fruit of Verlaine's very formal and proper year-long courtship. Published in 1870, again by Lemerre, the collection was not released until some two years later, at the conclusion of the Franco-Prussian War. Short pieces, for the most part, like their predecessors, they represent an important turning point in his art, in that the Parnassian element, superficial though it was in *Fêtes galantes,* is almost wholly absent, giving way to the rather conventional and (with only a few exceptions) somewhat forced effusions of the poet, happy to feel, or to convince himself that he felt, the joys and pangs of romantic love, and the anticipated pleasure of a settled middle-class married life, contrary to his still vague "saturnine" urges. That married life, however, despite the birth of a son, began to disintegrate almost as soon as it had begun.

❊

"Avant que tu ne t'en ailles…"

Avant que tu ne t'en ailles,
Pâle étoile du matin,
        —Mille cailles
Chantent, chantent dans le thym.—

Tourne devers le poète,
Dont les yeux sont pleins d'amour,
        —L'alouette
Monte au ciel avec le jour.—

Tourne ton regard que noie
L'aurore dans son azur;
        —Quelle joie
Parmi les champs de blé mûr!—

Puis fais luire ma pensée
Là-bas,—bien loin, oh! bien loin!
        —La rosée
Gaîment brille sur le foin.—

Dans le doux rêve où s'agite
Ma mie endormie encor…
        —Vite, vite,
Car voici le soleil d'or.—

v

"Morning star, before you pale…"

Morning star, before you pale
With the sunrise, daybreak bringing,
    —Myriad quail,
In the thyme, are singing, singing.—

Gaze upon this poet, mark
Well his love-abounding eyes.
    —Look! The lark
Rises in the morning skies.—

Gaze on him before your sight
Dims, in azure's dawning drowned;
    —What delight:
Fields of lush, ripe grain, all round!—

Then make thoughts of me shine through,
Far, there—oh so far away,
    —Bright, the dew
Gaily glistens on the hay.—

Into my love's reveries,
Restless as she lies, still sleeping…
    —Quickly, please!
See? The golden sun comes peeping!—

v

"*La lune blanche…*"

La lune blanche
Luit dans les bois;
De chaque branche
Part une voix
Sous la ramée…

Ô bien-aimée.

L'étang reflète,
Profond miroir,
La silhouette
Du saule noir
Où le vent pleure…

Rêvons, c'est l'heure.

Un vaste et tendre
Apaisement
Semble descendre
Du firmament
Que l'astre irise…

C'est l'heure exquise.

V I

"Among the trees…"

Among the trees
The moon gleams white,
Hushed repartees
Rustle tonight
From leaf and vine…

O mistress mine.

The inlet sleeps,
Deep in reflection:
Dark willow weeps
The wind's dejection.
Or so it seems…

The hour for dreams.

The heavens, star-lit,
Seem to bestow
Calm infinite
On earth below
From realms above…

The hour for love.

V I

"Une Sainte en son auréole..."

Une Sainte en son auréole,
Une Châtelaine en sa tour,
Tout ce que contient la parole
Humaine de grâce et d'amour;

La note d'or que fait entendre
Un cor dans le lointain des bois,
Mariée à la fierté tendre
Des nobles Dames d'autrefois;

Avec cela le charme insigne
D'un frais sourire triomphant
Éclos dans des candeurs de cygne
Et des rougeurs de femme-enfant;

Des aspects nacrés, blancs et roses,
Un doux accord patricien:
Je vois, j'entends toutes ces choses
Dans son nom Carlovingien.

V I I I

"A Saint set in her stained-glass glow…"

A Saint set in her stained-glass glow,
Milady in her castle tower,
All the sweet words that, here below,
Praise grace and sing love's gentle power;

The golden note that, distantly,
A woodland horn hums in our ear,
Wed to the tender dignity
Of noble Dames from yesteryear;

And, with it all, the charm, allure,
Of a smile fresh, triumphant, mild,
Sprung from the swan's hue—limpid, pure—
And blushings of a woman-child;

Visions of pink-pearl opaline,
Harmony of patrician airs…
I see, hear all these treasures in
That Carolingian name she bears.

V I I I

"J'allais par des chemins perfides…"

J'allais par des chemins perfides,
Douloureusement incertain.
Vos chères mains furent mes guides.

Si pâle à l'horizon lointain
Luisait un faible espoir d'aurore;
Votre regard fut le matin.

Nul bruit, sinon son pas sonore,
N'encourageait le voyageur.
Votre voix me dit: "Marche encore!"

Mon cœur craintif, mon sombre cœur
Pleurait, seul, sur la triste voie;
L'amour, délicieux vainqueur,

Nous a réunis dans la joie.

x x

"I used to wander aimlessly…"

I used to wander aimlessly,
Wanton my goal, grievous my plight.
Your dear hands led me, guided me.

Over the far horizon, night
Glowed with the pallid hope of dawn.
Your eyes' glance was my morning light.

No sound—save his own tread upon
The ground—to ease the wanderer's heart.
Your voice encouraged me: "Go on!"

Yes, my heart—dark, cowed, set apart,
Alone—bewailed its dire distress.
Sweet love, with its all-conquering art,

Joined us as one in joyousness.

x x

Romances sans paroles (1874)

S ince all poems, strictly speaking, are "words without
song," not the "songs without words" that Verlaine's
title announces, this title is doubly ironic in that the poems
(compositions?) of this collection are among the most musi-
cal in his repertoire, not only in their melodious play of
sounds, but also in the almost folk-
song-like form in which several of
them are written.

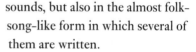

The period that produced these
poems was one of great upheaval:
social and political for France (and
for Paris in particular), following
Napoléon III's declaration of war
against Prussia; marital and emo-
tional for Verlaine, whose alco-
holism took little time translat-
ing itself into physical abuse
against his wife and infant son.
Although he was not left
unscathed by the political
events—as a Commune sympathizer, fearing retaliation, he
was obliged to move between several residences—it was, pre-
dictably, not those banal misfortunes that Verlaine turned
into his *romances,* but rather the shambles that his inner
urges, however he might want to repress them, made of his
young marriage. The immediate villain of the piece was

Arthur Rimbaud, the precocious visionary brat of a poet, whose admiration of the older Verlaine brought him to Paris at the latter's invitation, and into an impossible *ménage à trois*, where he intentionally scandalized and alienated all the proper bourgeois around him. Though Rimbaud was probably more a symptom than a cause, he soon completely captivated Verlaine, artistically and physically, precipitating, in short order, the poet's separation from Mathilde.

Divided into four short groupings—*Ariettes oubliées* (Forgotten Ariettas), *Paysages belges* (Belgian Landscapes), *Birds in the Night* (titled in English in the original), and *Aquarelles* (Watercolors)—*Romances sans paroles* was written between 1872 and 1873, and grew out of Verlaine's nostalgically colored recollections of an idealized life with Mathilde, on the one hand—a life tragically beyond his grasp—and lapidary impressionistic sketches of his turbulent, on-again off-again, year-long escapade through Belgium (and, eventually, to London) with his recalcitrant evil genius-*cum*-paramour. The collection was published in 1874 in the provincial town of Sens while Verlaine was imprisoned for the notorious flesh wound inflicted on Rimbaud during a lovers' skirmish in Brussels. A second edition would be brought out in 1887, at the height of Verlaine's celebrity, by his friend and frequent latter-day publisher Léon Vanier. Many of its poems remain among the most widely known, best loved, and artistically admired of his *œuvre*.

⁂

"C'est l'extase langoureuse…"

Le vent dans la plaine
Suspend son haleine.
Favart

C'est l'extase langoureuse,
C'est la fatigue amoureuse,
C'est tous les frissons des bois
Parmi l'étreinte des brises,
C'est, vers les ramures grises,
Le chœur des petites voix.

Ô le frêle et frais murmure!
Cela gazouille et susurre,
Cela ressemble au cri doux
Que l'herbe agitée expire…
Tu dirais, sous l'eau qui vire,
Le roulis sourd des cailloux.

Cette âme qui se lamente
En cette plainte dormante
C'est la nôtre, n'est-ce pas?
La mienne, dis, et la tienne,
Dont s'exhale l'humble antienne
Par ce tiède soir, tout bas?

ARIETTES OUBLIÉES, I

"It's the languorous ecstasy…"

The wind on the heath
Abates, holds its breath.
Favart

It's the languorous ecstasy,
It's the lovers' lethargy,
It's the rustling woods: the trees—
Branches, leaves, zephyr-caressed—
It's the dusk's gray-shadowed nest:
Hushed choir brustling in the breeze.

O that fragile rippling, whose
Whispered mutter trills and coos
Like the supple, tender sound
Wafting from the grasses, ruffled…
Or the river's pebbles, muffled,
Tumbling, soft, over the ground.

Ours, that soul lamenting, weeping
In that plaintive murmur, sleeping;
Ours it is, no? spirit twain—
Yours, mine—gently soughed and sighed
Low, this balmy eventide,
In a humble, soft refrain.

ARIETTES OUBLIÉES, I

"Il pleure dans mon cœur…"

Il pleut doucement sur la ville.
Arthur Rimbaud

Il pleure dans mon cœur
Comme il pleut sur la ville;
Quelle est cette langueur
Qui pénètre mon cœur?

Ô bruit doux de la pluie
Par terre et sur les toits!
Pour un cœur qui s'ennuie
Ô le chant de la pluie!

Il pleure sans raison
Dans ce cœur qui s'écœure.
Quoi! nulle trahison?…
Ce deuil est sans raison.

C'est bien la pire peine
De ne savoir pourquoi
Sans amour et sans haine
Mon cœur a tant de peine!

ARIETTES OUBLIÉES, III

"Like city's rain, my heart…"

The rain falls gently on the town.
Arthur Rimbaud

Like city's rain, my heart
Rains teardrops too. What now,
This languorous ache, this smart
That pierces, wounds my heart?

Gentle, the sound of rain
Pattering roof and ground!
Ah, for the heart in pain,
Sweet is the sound of rain!

Tears rain—but who knows why?—
And fill my heartsick heart.
No faithless lover's lie?…
It mourns, and who knows why?

And nothing pains me so—
With neither love nor hate—
As simply not to know
Why my heart suffers so.

ARIETTES OUBLIÉES, III

"Le piano que baise une main frêle…"

Son joyeux, importun, d'un clavecin sonore.
Pétrus Borel

Le piano que baise une main frêle
Luit dans le soir rose et gris vaguement,
Tandis qu'avec un très léger bruit d'aile
Un air bien vieux, bien faible et bien charmant
Rôde discret, épeuré quasiment,
Par le boudoir longtemps parfumé d'Elle.

Qu'est-ce que c'est que ce berceau soudain
Qui lentement dorlote mon pauvre être?
Que voudrais-tu de moi, doux Chant badin?
Qu'as-tu voulu, fin refrain incertain
Qui vas tantôt mourir vers la fenêtre
Ouverte un peu sur le petit jardin?

ARIETTES OUBLIÉES, V

"Bright in the evening's gray and pinkish blur..."

Gay, nagging sound of sonorous harpsichord.
Pétrus Borel

Bright in the evening's gray and pinkish blur,
A piano stands, kissed by a slight, frail hand,
While, like the whisper of a wing astir,
An air from long ago—faint, obscure, and
Yet fair—haunts the boudoir as if it were
Fearful to tread midst the perfume of Her.

What is this cradle that, now, suddenly
Rocks my poor body, lulls my being? Why?
What do you want, mischievous Melody,
Sweet, muted strain? What would you do with me,
You, who will soon be dying, over by
The window open on the greenery?

ARIETTES OUBLIÉES, V

"Ô triste, triste était mon âme…"

Ô triste, triste était mon âme
À cause, à cause d'une femme.

Je ne me suis pas consolé
Bien que mon cœur s'en soit allé,

Bien que mon cœur, bien que mon âme
Eussent fui loin de cette femme.

Je ne me suis pas consolé,
Bien que mon cœur s'en soit allé.

Et mon cœur, mon cœur trop sensible
Dit à mon âme: Est-il possible,

Est-il possible,—le fût-il,—
Ce fier exil, ce triste exil?

Mon âme dit à mon cœur: Sais-je
Moi-même que nous veut ce piège

D'être présents bien qu'exilés,
Encore que loin en allés?

ARIETTES OUBLIÉES, VII

"So sad my heart, so sad it was…"

So sad my heart, so sad it was,
And woman, woman was the cause.

My heart flew from her side—but oh,
I knew no solace for my woe.

No solace for my soul, my heart,
Though they and she were far apart.

My heart flew from her side—but oh,
I knew no solace for my woe;

A woe that pained my heart. And he
Said to my soul: "Soul, can it be?

What? Can it be that you and I
Are exiles? We two, exiles? Why?"

And my soul answered. "See?" he said.
"See what a clever trap she's laid!

She makes us think we're free, and yet
She lets us flee… but not forget."

ARIETTES OUBLIÉES, VII

"Dans l'interminable…"

Dans l'interminable
Ennui de la plaine
La neige incertaine
Luit comme du sable.

Le ciel est de cuivre
Sans lueur aucune.
On croirait voir vivre
Et mourir la lune.

Comme des nuées
Flottent gris les chênes
Des forêts prochaines
Parmi les buées.

Le ciel est de cuivre
Sans lueur aucune.
On croirait voir vivre
Et mourir la lune.

Corneille poussive
Et vous, les loups maigres,
Par ces bises aigres
Quoi donc vous arrive?

"Covering the land…"

Covering the land—
Dismal, endless plain—
Blurring the terrain,
Snow haze gleams like sand.

Bronze the sky, with no
Glimmering of light:
Is the moon to grow
Dim, and die tonight?

In the woods, close by,
Billows the fog, cloaks
Gray the cloud-like oaks
Floating on the sky.

Bronze the sky, with no
Glimmering of light:
Is the moon to grow
Dim, and die tonight?

Scrawny wolves, and you,
Wheezing ravens, when
Winds blow sharp, what then?
What? What can you do?

Dans l'interminable
Ennui de la plaine
La neige incertaine
Luit comme du sable.

Covering the land—
Dismal, endless plain—
Blurring the terrain,
Snow haze gleams like sand.

"*L'ombre des arbres dans la rivière embrumée...*"

Le rossignol qui du haut d'une branche se regarde dedans,
croit être tombé dans la rivière. Il est au sommet d'un chêne
et toutefois il a peur de se noyer. *Cyrano de Bergerac*

L'ombre des arbres dans la rivière embrumée
    Meurt comme de la fumée
Tandis qu'en l'air, parmi les ramures réelles,
    Se plaignent les tourterelles.

Combien, ô voyageur, ce paysage blême
    Te mira blême toi-même,
Et que tristes pleuraient dans les hautes feuillées
    Tes espérances noyées!

M A I , J U I N 1 8 7 2 . / I X

"Reflections in the fogbound rivulet..."

The nightingale, looking into the stream from a high branch,
thinks he has fallen into it. He is perched atop an oak, yet
fears he may drown. *Cyrano de Bergerac*

Reflections in the fogbound rivulet,
      Tree-shadows die like smoke. And yet,
Turtledoves perch atop the living trees,
      Cooing their plaintive melodies.

How often, traveler, have you seen your blear
      Image reflected in life's drear,
Bleak scene, while high above, midst bough and leaf,
      Your drowned hopes, wailful, weep their grief!

MAY, JUNE 1872. / IX

Walcourt

Briques et tuiles,
Ô les charmants
Petits asiles
Pour les amants!

Houblons et vignes,
Feuilles et fleurs,
Tentes insignes
Des francs buveurs!

Guinguettes claires,
Bières, clameurs,
Servantes chères
À tous fumeurs!

Gares prochaines,
Gais chemins grands…
Quelles aubaines,
Bons juifs-errants!

JUILLET 72. / PAYSAGES BELGES

Walcourt

Bricks, tiles... How sweet
Such cozy cover,
Charming retreat
For man and lover!

Plants, flowers, vines,
Hops in the pot,
Awnings and signs
To lure the sot!

Bright taverns, beer,
Bustle and brawl,
Tap-wenches, dear
To smokers all!

Train stations there,
Gay avenues...
What pleasures rare,
My Wandering Jews!

JULY 72. / PAYSAGES BELGES

Charleroi

Dans l'herbe noire
Les Kobolds vont.
Le vent profond
Pleure, on veut croire.

Quoi donc se sent?
L'avoine siffle.
Un buisson gifle
L'œil au passant.

Plutôt des bouges
Que des maisons.
Quels horizons
De forges rouges!

On sent donc quoi?
Des gares tonnent,
Les yeux s'étonnent,
Où Charleroi?

Parfums sinistres!
Qu'est-ce que c'est?
Quoi bruissait
Comme des sistres?

Charleroi

The Kobolds come!
Grass, black. And deep
The winds. They weep.
Or so think some.

That odor. Why?
Fields of oats, whistling.
And brambles bristling
Against the eye.

Not houses, sties,
Hovels. And more,
Forges galore.
Red glow the skies!

Smells? *Oh là là!*
Noise? Trains growl past.
Our eyes, aghast.
This? Charleroi…?

Stenches abounding!
What's that? What is
That whir? That whiz?
Like sistrum sounding?

Sites brutaux!
Oh! votre haleine,
Sueur humaine,
Cris des métaux!

Dans l'herbe noire
Les Kobolds vont.
Le vent profond
Pleure, on veut croire.

PAYSAGES BELGES

Dens, brutal, reeking!
Your breath, a debt
Of human sweat,
Hot metals shrieking!

The Kobolds come!
Grass, black. And deep
The winds. They weep.
Or so think some.

PAYSAGES BELGES

Green

Voici des fruits, des fleurs, des feuilles et des branches
Et puis voici mon cœur qui ne bat que pour vous.
Ne le déchirez pas avec vos deux mains blanches
Et qu'à vos yeux si beaux l'humble présent soit doux.

J'arrive tout couvert encore de rosée
Que le vent du matin vient glacer à mon front.
Souffrez que ma fatigue à vos pieds reposée
Rêve des chers instants qui la délasseront.

Sur votre jeune sein laissez rouler ma tête
Toute sonore encor de vos derniers baisers;
Laissez-la s'apaiser de la bonne tempête,
Et que je dorme un peu puisque vous reposez.

AQUARELLES

Green

Here, take these boughs, leaves, fruits, and flowers. And take
This heart that beats for you alone. Take care
Lest, taking, with those soft, white hands, you break
This humble gift I pray your eyes find fair.

To you I come, still cloaked with morning dew,
Breeze-frozen on my brow. Ah, let me, please,
Lie at your feet, dream of the times we knew:
Precious those times, restful their memories.

Let my head, filled with kisses echoing yet,
Loll on the fresh, young beauty of your breast;
Let it find calm above love's storm, and let
Me sleep a little, even as you rest.

AQUARELLES

Spleen

Les roses étaient toutes rouges
Et les lierres étaient tout noirs.

Chère, pour peu que tu te bouges,
Renaissent tous mes désespoirs.

Le ciel était trop bleu, trop tendre,
La mer trop verte et l'air trop doux.

Je crains toujours,—ce qu'est d'attendre!—
Quelque fuite atroce de vous.

Du houx à la feuille vernie
Et du luisant buis je suis las,

Et de la campagne infinie
Et de tout, fors de vous, hélas!

AQUARELLES

Spleen

The roses were the reddest red,
The ivy vines the blackest black.

You merely move, and deep my dread,
And, dark, my woes come springing back.

Too blue, too gentle was the sky,
The air too sweet, too green the sea.

I fear, I languish... ah! lest I
See you betray me, flee from me.

To holly bright and mistletoe
Of shining leaf I bid adieu,

To nature's boring realm, and—oh!—
To everything, alas, but you.

AQUARELLES

Streets I

Dansons la gigue!

J'aimais surtout ses jolis yeux,
Plus clairs que l'étoile des cieux,
J'aimais ses yeux malicieux.

Dansons la gigue!

Elle avait des façons vraiment
De désoler un pauvre amant,
Que c'en était vraiment charmant!

Dansons la gigue!

Mais je trouve encore meilleur
Le baiser de sa bouche en fleur
Depuis qu'elle est morte à mon cœur.

Dansons la gigue!

Je me souviens, je me souviens
Des heures et des entretiens,
Et c'est le meilleur de mes biens.

Dansons la gigue!

Streets I

Let's dance a jig!

I loved above all else her eyes,
Brighter than stars that light the skies,
I loved her eyes that tantalize.

Let's dance a jig!

She had that manner... Ah, but it
Could make poor lovers lose their wit,
Yet charm them too, I must admit!

Let's dance a jig!

And even more, today, I miss
Her lips pursed in a flower-kiss—
Now dead and gone, alas, the bliss.

Let's dance a jig!

And memories, my memories...
Hours spent in tender colloquies...
Of all my wealth, most precious these.

Let's dance a jig!

SOHO. / AQUARELLES

Streets II

Ô la rivière dans la rue !
Fantastiquement apparue
Derrière un mur haut de cinq pieds,
Elle roule sans un murmure
Son onde opaque et pourtant pure
Par les faubourgs pacifiés.

La chaussée est très large, en sorte
Que l'eau jaune comme une morte
Dévale ample et sans nuls espoirs
De rien refléter que la brume,
Même alors que l'aurore allume
Les cottages jaunes et noirs.

PADDINGTON. / AQUARELLES

Streets II

Strange river, sprung from who knows where!
It streams along a thoroughfare
Behind a five-foot wall, without
A murmur; dim, opaque, and yet
A pure, unsullied rivulet,
Coursing the precincts roundabout

The peaceful, sleeping countryside.
Its death-gray water, running wide
Along the roadway, hopeless, flows;
Its sole reflection: fog and mist,
Even as daybreak's glow has kissed
The black and yellow bungalows.

PADDINGTON. / AQUARELLES

Sagesse (1881)

*V*erlaine's penitential sincerity in writing the twenty-one "conversion" poems of *Sagesse* is not, nor should it be, a point at issue. No doubt he thought himself sincere in his yearning for the "wisdom" of the title when he first began penning them in his Belgian prison cell, originally intending them for a collection to be entitled, appropriately, *Cellulairement* ("Confinementally"), and throughout their composition. And no doubt he certainly meant to be, as the impassioned breast-beating in his preface to the first edition makes clear, condemning, as it does, the "vers sceptiques et tristement légers" (the skeptical [i.e. "irreligious"] and sadly lighthearted verses) of his misspent youth.

But sincerity and aspirations toward a spiritual renewal aside, if this collection, thought masterful by some and banal by others, were the only one Verlaine had ever written, I doubt very much that he would, today, enjoy his preeminent rank in modern French, and world, poetry. I suspect that he would be considered only a very competent, second-rank poet of well-structured but unexciting religious verse, not especially original in form, style, or content, bland and often even maudlin, destined to be studied by literature graduate students and, perhaps, seminarians. He would not be thought of as an exceptional poetic innovator, nor would his name evoke the qualities of musicality, verbal elegance, formal variety, and stylistic fancy—even a goodly dose of capriciousness and whimsy—that are the legacy of his earlier collections and that surface here and there in his later ones.

Great sinners and great saints are often cut from the same cloth; or, to mix a metaphor, are often two sides of the same coin. In Verlaine's case, noble intentions notwithstanding, once released from prison, his life was to be a continual backslide into debauch, relieved, for a time, by doubtlessly sincere but short-lived and ineffectual attempts at reform. Reconciled off and on with Rimbaud—and with his ever-forgiving mother, who had long suffered his excesses, physically as well as emotionally—but never to be reconciled with Mathilde, he completed the manuscript of *Sagesse* in England, where he taught French in a variety of institutions, with notable lack of success. (A number of the poems included had, indeed, been written earlier and were eventually tailored to fit the new mood.) The volume was not published until two years later, by a Catholic press. As with his previous volumes, publication was at his own expense. Vanier would, however, publish a second, revised, edition in 1889.

❋

"Beauté des femmes, leur faiblesse, et ces mains pâles…"

Beauté des femmes, leur faiblesse, et ces mains pâles
Qui font souvent le bien et peuvent tout le mal,
Et ces yeux, où plus rien ne reste d'animal
Que juste assez pour dire: "assez" aux fureurs mâles!

Et toujours, maternelle endormeuse des râles,
Même quand elle ment, cette voix! Matinal
Appel, ou chant bien doux à vêpre, ou frais signal,
Ou beau sanglot qui va mourir au pli des châles!…

Hommes durs! Vie atroce et laide d'ici-bas!
Ah! que du moins, loin des baisers et des combats,
Quelque chose demeure un peu sur la montagne,

Quelque chose du cœur enfantin et subtil,
Bonté, respect! Car, qu'est-ce qui nous accompagne,
Et vraiment, quand la mort viendra, que reste-t-il?

I , V

"Beauty of women, weakness, pale soft skin…"

Beauty of women, weakness, pale soft skin
Of hands that do much good, yet can do all
Our ill; and, last trace of the beast withal,
Eyes to say "stop" to furors masculine!

Ever that voice that soothes every chagrin;
Maternal, even when it lies; sweet call
Of morning, evensong, sobs in a shawl,
Sweet muffled sighs, or dalliance feminine!…

Men, harsh! Life, vile and ugly here below!
At least, far, far from love and battle's woe,
Let something tender, childlike linger on

The peak: kindness, respect! For what do we
Take with us when we go? And, finally,
When death arrives, what lasts when we are gone?

I , V

"Un grand sommeil noir…"

Un grand sommeil noir
Tombe sur ma vie:
Dormez, tout espoir,
Dormez, toute envie!

Je ne vois plus rien,
Je perds la mémoire
Du mal et du bien…
Ô la triste histoire!

Je suis un berceau
Qu'une main balance
Au creux d'un caveau:
Silence, silence!

I I I ,   V

"A vast, black lethargy…"

A vast, black lethargy
  Damps my life's fire:
Sleep, sleep, all hope, and free
  Me of desire!

Dim now has grown my sight,
  No more can I
Remember wrong from right…
  Sad tale, awry!

A cradle am I, deep
  Beneath the ground;
A hand rocks me to sleep:
  No sound, no sound!

III, V

"Le ciel est, par-dessus le toit…"

Le ciel est, par-dessus le toit,
      Si bleu, si calme!
Un arbre, par-dessus le toit,
      Berce sa palme.

La cloche, dans le ciel qu'on voit,
      Doucement tinte.
Un oiseau sur l'arbre qu'on voit
      Chante sa plainte.

Mon Dieu, mon Dieu, la vie est là,
      Simple et tranquille.
Cette paisible rumeur-là
      Vient de la ville.

—Qu'as-tu fait, ô toi que voilà
      Pleurant sans cesse,
Dis, qu'as-tu fait, toi que voilà,
      De ta jeunesse?

I I I , V I

"Above the roof the sky is fair…"

Above the roof the sky is fair;
      Blue, calm, serene.
A tree branch sways… The sky is fair,
      Tranquil the scene.

A bell, in that sky, fills the air
      With sweet content.
A bird, in that tree, fills the air
      With sad lament.

My God, my God, out there… That's where
      Real life is found.
A simple town… And everywhere,
      Its gentle sound.

"What have you done, you, weeping there
      Your endless tears?
Tell me, what have you done, you there,
      With youth's best years?"

I I I , V I

"Le son du cor s'afflige vers les bois…"

Le son du cor s'afflige vers les bois
D'une douleur on veut croire orpheline
Qui vient mourir au bas de la colline
Parmi la bise errant en courts abois.

L'âme du loup pleure dans cette voix
Qui monte avec le soleil qui décline
D'une agonie on veut croire câline
Et qui ravit et qui navre à la fois.

Pour faire mieux cette plainte assoupie,
La neige tombe à longs traits de charpie
À travers le couchant sanguinolent,

Et l'air a l'air d'être un soupir d'automne,
Tant il fait doux par ce soir monotone
Où se dorlote un paysage lent.

III,   IX

"The horn's sound in the wood sobs dolefully…"

The horn's sound in the wood sobs dolefully
With woe one hopes an orphan, come to die
At the hill's foot, and say its last goodbye
In gentle gusts of crisp cacophony.

And in that voice, the wolf-soul's agony,
And tears one hopes benign; voice rising high
As lower, lower the sun sets in the sky;
Agony that both charms and tortures me.

To make this hushed lament more peaceful still,
The snow slashes amid the winter chill,
Shredding the blood-red sunset, as the air

Sighs with a sigh more like the autumn's; and
So evening falls, soft, calm, and everywhere
Spreads, languid, its caress over the land.

III, IX

"*La bise se rue à travers…*"

La bise se rue à travers
Les buissons tout noirs et tout verts,
Glaçant la neige éparpillée
Dans la campagne ensoleillée.
L'odeur est aigre près des bois,
L'horizon chante avec des voix,
Les coqs des clochers des villages
Luisent crûment sur les nuages.
C'est délicieux de marcher
À travers ce brouillard léger
Qu'un vent taquin parfois retrousse.
Ah! fi de mon vieux feu qui tousse!
J'ai des fourmis plein les talons.
Debout, mon âme, vite, allons!
C'est le printemps sévère encore,
Mais qui par instant s'édulcore
D'un souffle tiède juste assez
Pour mieux sentir les froids passés
Et penser au Dieu de clémence…
Va, mon âme, à l'espoir immense!

III, XI

"The wind whips through the bushes, green…"

The wind whips through the bushes, green
And black, freezing a frosty sheen
Over the sunlit snows spread round.
From the horizon comes the sound
Of voices; bitter, redolent,
Rises the woodland's heady scent;
Gleaming, the village weathercocks,
Atop the steeples, bell towers, clocks,
Glare on the clouds. What joy, what bliss
It is to amble on like this,
Rambling through mist and fog, whose skirt,
At times, the roguish breeze, a-flirt,
Hoists to her knees! Bah! No need now
For my old sputtering fire! Ah, how
I tingle with desire to wander
Footloose and free. Up, soul! Out yonder
Spring warms her breath—but just a whit,
Lest we forget the cold—for it
Bespeaks God's tender mercy… Come,
My soul, trust in His glorydom!

I I I ,   X I

"L'échelonnement des haies…"

L'échelonnement des haies
Moutonne à l'infini, mer
Claire dans le brouillard clair
Qui sent bon les jeunes baies.

Des arbres et des moulins
Sont légers sur le vert tendre
Où vient s'ébattre et s'étendre
L'agilité des poulains.

Dans ce vague d'un Dimanche
Voici se jouer aussi
De grandes brebis aussi
Douces que leur laine blanche.

Tout à l'heure déferlait
L'onde, roulée en volutes,
De cloches comme des flûtes
Dans le ciel comme du lait.

STICKNEY, 75. / III, XIII

"The hedges billow like the sea's…"

The hedges billow like the sea's
Whitecaps of fleece, ocean unending,
On, on… Bright in the bright haze, blending
Mists with the scents of laurel trees.

Windmill and branch laze airily
Over the tender grasses where
Colts caper, frolic here and there,
Boundless in youthful energy.

Here in this Sunday morning full
Of dim obscurities, comes, too,
Many a robust, playful ewe,
Soft as the whiteness of her wool.

Just now there went unfurling, high
Above, swirling to heaven, the sound
Of bells, like flutes, all whirling round,
Up, up, into the milk-white sky.

STICKNEY, 75. / III, XIII

"La 'grande ville'! Un tas criard de
pierres blanches…"

La "grande ville"! Un tas criard de pierres blanches
Où rage le soleil comme en pays conquis.
Tous les vices ont leurs tanières, les exquis
Et les hideux, dans ce désert de pierres blanches.

Des odeurs. Des bruits vains. Où que vague le cœur,
Toujours ce poudroiement vertigineux de sable,
Toujours ce remuement de la chose coupable
Dans cette solitude où s'écœure le cœur!

De près, de loin, le Sage aura sa Thébaïde
Parmi le fade ennui qui monte de ceci,
D'autant plus âpre et plus sanctifiante aussi
Que deux parts de son âme y pleurent, dans ce vide!

PARIS, 77. / III, XVI

" 'The city!' Gaudy cluster of white stones…"

"The city!" Gaudy cluster of white stones,
Where the sun seethes, as in a conquered land.
Each vice has its own lair—the fair, the bland,
The odious—in this desert of white stones.

Smells. Empty sounds. Wherever roams the heart,
Always that crumbling, dizzying sand, that sin
Whirring about its whirlwind guilt within
This solitude of the disheartened heart!

Near, far, the Sage yearns for his desert too
Among this emptiness and dour ennui,
All the more bleak, yet sacrosanct, for he
Harbors a soul, racked, weeping, rent in two.

PARIS, 77. / III, XVI

Jadis et naguère (1884)

*P*resenting somewhat the appearance of a miscellany, the
works of "yesteryear" and "not long since" that com-
prise, respectively, the volume *Jadis et naguère,* unlike its pre-
decessors, offer no unified theme other than that of their
temporal disparity of composition. Including several poems
first written for *Cellulairement,* and even a one-act Wat-
teauesque verse comedy of *Fêtes galantes* inspiration, the col-
lection, pulled together for reasons monetary as much as (if
not more than) artistic, is admittedly uneven in quality as
well as in content.

Returning to Paris in 1882 after almost ten years of
sojourns outside the capital—his prison stay in Belgium,
teaching posts in England and France, and even a doomed
attempt at bucolic life and farming in the provinces—Ver-
laine sought, at first with only moderate success, to reinstate
himself into the literary world that had begun to forget him.
The death from typhoid of a student-protégé, Lucien Léti-
nois, whom he had taken under his wing and for whom he
tried to convince himself that he had only a paternal con-
cern, was devastating to his fragile psyche. It was perhaps
the catalyst, if one was really needed, for an unbridled lapse
into the excesses of alcohol and indiscriminate sex: the for-
mer, leading eventually to another prison stay (two months
in the town of Vouziers for several violent physical attacks
against his mother); the latter, helping, along with assorted
lawsuits, virtually to impoverish him thanks to the seamy

relationships he engaged in with unscrupulous casual partners. His finances were strained further when Mathilde and her vindictive family took advantage of the new divorce law to end his marriage beyond hope of repair.

Jadis et naguère was brought out at the beginning of 1885, still at Verlaine's own expense, by Léon Vanier, who would, however, eventually publish others of Verlaine's collections without the customary subvention, whether out of friendship, pity, or artistic conviction. For all its flaws, it cannot be ignored. While the second part, aside from its almost Baudelairean prologue, is ponderous in the extreme, the first—comprising the twenty varied poems of *Sonnets et autres vers* (Sonnets and Other Verses), the comedy *Les Uns et les autres* (The Ones and the Others), the half-dozen often rhetorical works of *Vers jeunes* (Youthful Verses), and the nine, very stylized, of *À la manière de plusieurs* (In the Manner of Several Others)—contains a few "classic" pieces from the Verlaine repertoire. The poems "Art poétique" and "Langueur," especially, had helped restore him to prominence among his contemporaries: established literati like the important Décadent novelist J.-K. Huysmans, as well as younger writers for whom he was becoming an artistically respected, almost legendary (if morally dubious) inspiration.

❃

Pierrot

À Léon Valade

Ce n'est plus le rêveur lunaire du vieil air
Qui riait aux aïeux dans les dessus de porte;
Sa gaîté, comme sa chandelle, hélas! est morte,
Et son spectre aujourd'hui nous hante, mince et clair.

Et voici que parmi l'effroi d'un long éclair
Sa pâle blouse a l'air, au vent froid qui l'emporte,
D'un linceul, et sa bouche est béante, de sorte
Qu'il semble hurler sous les morsures du ver.

Avec le bruit d'un vol d'oiseaux de nuit qui passe,
Ses manches blanches font vaguement par l'espace
Des signes fous auxquels personne ne répond.

Ses yeux sont deux grands trous où rampe du phosphore
Et la farine rend plus effroyable encore
Sa face exsangue au nez pointu de moribond.

SONNETS ET AUTRES VERS (JADIS)

Pierrot

For Léon Valade

No more the old song's moonlight dreamer he,
Leering from wood-carved portals overhead.
His joy, alas! is, like his candle, dead;
Today his ghost, translucent, haunts us. See,

There, in a frightful lightning flash, blown free,
His pale blouse, wind-swept, like a shroud outspread;
See, there, his mouth agape, his look of dread,
As if to howl his worm-gnawed agony.

With whir of nightbirds winging past, his white
Sleeves beat the air in frantic gestures, quite
Aimless and vague, with none to answer him.

His eyes are two deep holes of phosphorous;
And whiteface makes ever more hideous
That sharp-nosed near-death mask, so ghastly, grim.

SONNETS ET AUTRES VERS (JADIS)

Le Squelette

À Albert Mérat

Deux reîtres saouls, courant les champs, virent parmi
La fange d'un fossé profond, une carcasse
Humaine dont la faim torve d'un loup fugace
Venait de disloquer l'ossature à demi.

La tête, intacte, avait un rictus ennemi
Qui nous attriste, nous énerve et nous agace.
Or, peu mystiques, nos capitaines Fracasse
Songèrent (John Falstaff lui-même en eût frémi)

Qu'ils avaient bu, que tout vin bu filtre et s'égoutte,
Et qu'en outre ce mort avec son chef béant
Ne serait pas fâché de boire aussi, sans doute.

Mais comme il ne faut pas insulter au Néant,
Le squelette s'étant dressé sur son séant
Fit signe qu'ils pouvaient continuer leur route.

SONNETS ET AUTRES VERS (JADIS)

The Skeleton

For Albert Mérat

Two boisterous ruffians, a besotted pair,
Riding, came on a ditch with muck piled high,
On which a human carcass caught their eye,
De-boned by some starveling rogue wolf; yet there,

Intact, the head, frozen in death's grim stare,
Remained: fierce grin, morose, unnerving. (Why,
Falstaff himself would have been stunned thereby.)
Our roisterers, not given much to prayer

Or piety, thought only of their schnapps—
Imbibed, digested, ready now to flow:
The corpse, agape, would like a drink, perhaps!

Impious thought, and most malapropos!
Up sits the skeleton and lets our chaps
Know with a gesture that they're free to go!

SONNETS ET AUTRES VERS (JADIS)

Art poétique

À Charles Morice

De la musique avant toute chose,
Et pour cela préfère l'Impair
Plus vague et plus soluble dans l'air,
Sans rien en lui qui pèse ou qui pose.

Il faut aussi que tu n'ailles point
Choisir tes mots sans quelque méprise:
Rien de plus cher que la chanson grise
Où l'Indécis au Précis se joint.

C'est des beaux yeux derrière des voiles,
C'est le grand jour tremblant de midi,
C'est, par un ciel d'automne attiédi,
Le bleu fouillis des claires étoiles!

Car nous voulons la Nuance encor,
Pas la Couleur, rien que la nuance!
Oh! la nuance seule fiance
Le rêve au rêve et la flûte au cor!

Fuis du plus loin la Pointe assassine,
L'Esprit cruel et le Rire impur,
Qui font pleurer les yeux de l'Azur,
Et tout cet ail de basse cuisine!

Ars Poetica

For Charles Morice

Music first and foremost! In your verse,
Choose those meters odd of syllable,
Supple in the air, vague, flexible,
Free of pounding beat, heavy or terse.

Choose the words you use—now right, now wrong—
With abandon: when the poet's vision
Couples the Precise with Imprecision,
Best the giddy shadows of his song:

Eyes veiled, hidden, dark with mystery,
Sunshine trembling in the noonday glare,
Starlight, in the tepid autumn air,
Shimmering in night-blue filigree!

For Nuance, not Color absolute,
Is your goal; subtle and shaded hue!
Nuance! It alone is what lets you
Marry dream to dream, and horn to flute!

Shun all cruel and ruthless Railleries;
Hurtful Quip, lewd Laughter, that appall
Heaven, Azure-eyed, to tears; and all
Garlic-stench scullery recipes!

Prends l'éloquence et tords-lui son cou!
Tu feras bien, en train d'énergie,
De rendre un peu la Rime assagie.
Si l'on n'y veille, elle ira jusqu'où?

Ô qui dira les torts de la Rime?
Quel enfant sourd ou quel nègre fou
Nous a forgé ce bijou d'un sou
Qui sonne creux et faux sous la lime?

De la musique encore et toujours!
Que ton vers soit la chose envolée
Qu'on sent qui fuit d'une âme en allée
Vers d'autres cieux à d'autres amours.

Que ton vers soit la bonne aventure
Éparse au vent crispé du matin
Qui va fleurant la menthe et le thym…
Et tout le reste est littérature.

SONNETS ET AUTRES VERS (JADIS)

Take vain Eloquence and wring its neck!
Best you keep your Rhyme sober and sound,
Lest it wander, reinless and unbound—
How far? Who can say?—if not in check!

Rhyme! Who will its infamies revile?
What deaf child, what Black of little wit
Forged this worthless bauble, fashioned it
False and hollow-sounding to the file?

Music first and foremost, and forever!
Let your verse be what goes soaring, sighing,
Set free, fleeing from the soul gone flying
Off to other skies and loves, wherever.

Let your verse be aimless chance, delighting
In good-omened fortune, sprinkled over
Dawn's wind, bristling scents of mint, thyme, clover…
All the rest is nothing more than writing.

SONNETS ET AUTRES VERS (JADIS)

Allégorie

À Jules Valadon

Despotique, pesant, incolore, l'Été,
Comme un roi fainéant présidant un supplice,
S'étire par l'ardeur blanche du ciel complice
Et bâille. L'homme dort loin du travail quitté.

L'alouette au matin, lasse, n'a pas chanté,
Pas un nuage, pas un souffle, rien qui plisse
Ou ride cet azur implacablement lisse
Où le silence bout dans l'immobilité.

L'âpre engourdissement a gagné les cigales
Et sur leur lit étroit de pierres inégales
Les ruisseaux à moitié taris ne sautent plus.

Une rotation incessante de moires
Lumineuses étend ses flux et ses reflux...
Des guêpes, çà et là, volent, jaunes et noires.

SONNETS ET AUTRES VERS (JADIS)

Allegory

For Jules Valadon

Despotic Summer, heavy, colorless—
Like king presiding tortures, fey, effete—
Yawns, stretches in the scheming skies' pale heat;
Man sleeps the sleep of labor's sweet recess.

The lark lay hushed: too tiring her distress.
No cloud, no breath of air: a calm complete.
No wrinkle in the sky's relentless sheet
Of blue, seething in torpor's mute caress.

The crickets, numbed to lethargy, are lying
Still. In their pebbled beds the brooklets, drying,
Billow and bound about no more. A flowing,

Ebbing of opalescence flecks the air,
Shimmering in its iridescence, glowing…
Black, yellow dragonflies dart here, dart there.

SONNETS ET AUTRES VERS (JADIS)

Circonspection

À Gaston Sénéchal

Donne ta main, retiens ton souffle, asseyons-nous
Sous cet arbre géant où vient mourir la brise
En soupirs inégaux sous la ramure grise
Que caresse le clair de lune blême et doux.

Immobiles, baissons nos yeux vers nos genoux.
Ne pensons pas, rêvons. Laissons faire à leur guise
Le bonheur qui s'enfuit et l'amour qui s'épuise,
Et nos cheveux frôlés par l'aile des hiboux.

Oublions d'espérer. Discrète et contenue,
Que l'âme de chacun de nous deux continue
Ce calme et cette mort sereine du soleil.

Restons silencieux parmi la paix nocturne:
Il n'est pas bon d'aller troubler dans son sommeil
La nature, ce dieu féroce et taciturne.

SONNETS ET AUTRES VERS (JADIS)

Circumspection

For Gaston Sénéchal

Give me your hand, hold still your breath, let's sit
Beneath this great tree, where the dusk-gray air
Wafts sighing, dying in the boughs, and where
The pale leaves softly stir, caressed, moon-lit.

Motionless, let us bow our heads and quit
All thought. Let's dream our dream, let's leave to their
Devices joy and love—windswept—like hair
Breeze-blown, brushed by the owl's wing grazing it.

Let us not even hope. In quiet peace
Let our two souls mirror the day's surcease
And the sun's death in night, tranquil and deep.

In silence let us rest, calm, resolute:
It is not right to trouble, in his sleep,
Nature, that fearsome god, ferocious, mute.

SONNETS ET AUTRES VERS (JADIS)

Langueur

À Georges Courteline

Je suis l'Empire à la fin de la décadence,
Qui regarde passer les grands Barbares blancs
En composant des acrostiches indolents
D'un style d'or où la langueur du soleil danse.

L'âme seulette a mal au cœur d'un ennui dense.
Là-bas on dit qu'il est de longs combats sanglants.
Ô n'y pouvoir, étant si faible aux vœux si lents,
Ô n'y vouloir fleurir un peu cette existence!

Ô n'y vouloir, ô n'y pouvoir mourir un peu!
Ah! tout est bu! Bathylle, as-tu fini de rire?
Ah! tout est bu, tout est mangé! Plus rien à dire!

Seul, un poème un peu niais qu'on jette au feu,
Seul, un esclave un peu coureur qui vous néglige,
Seul, un ennui d'on ne sait quoi qui vous afflige!

À LA MANIÈRE DE PLUSIEURS, II (JADIS)

Languor

For Georges Courteline

I am the Empire as the decadence
Draws to a close: midst Vandals' conquest, I
Compose my fey rhymes, my acrostics wry,
A-dance with languid, sun-gilt indolence.

A dense ennui sickens my soul, my sense.
I'm told that bloody battles rage hard by:
Why can I not—slow, flaccid-witted—why
Will I not flower, a bit, life's impotence?

Why can I—will I—not die just a bit!
Ah! Nothing left to drink? You laugh, Bathyllus!
Nothing to say! No food, no drink to fill us!

Only a poem; into the fire with it!
Only a randy slave to let you languish;
Only a vague ennui's dim, obscure anguish.

À LA MANIÈRE DE PLUSIEURS, II (JADIS)

Prologue

Ce sont choses crépusculaires,
Des visions de fin de nuit.
Ô Vérité, tu les éclaires
Seulement d'une aube qui luit

Si pâle dans l'ombre abhorrée
Qu'on doute encore par instants
Si c'est la lune qui les crée
Sous l'horreur des rameaux flottants,

Ou si ces fantômes moroses
Vont tout à l'heure prendre corps
Et se mêler au chœur des choses
Dans les harmonieux décors

Du soleil et de la nature;
Doux à l'homme et proclamant Dieu
Pour l'extase de l'hymne pure
Jusqu'à la douceur du ciel bleu.

NAGUÈRE

Prologue

Dim-lit, those visions born of night,
Of twilight moments just before
The Dawn: O Truth, your pallid light
Grays them in loathsome shades; the more

One looks, the more one wonders whether
It is the moonglow that endows
Those forms with life, coming together
Beneath the frightening, swaying boughs,

Or if those doleful specters will
Take shape in gentle brightenings
Of day, little by little, till
They mingle with that choir of things

That nature's sunlit harmony—
Proclaiming God, delighting man—
Sings in pure hymns of ecstasy
Unto the heavens' blue-arching span.

N A G U È R E

Amour (1888)

*W*ithout the ambivalent but somewhat stabilizing influence of his mother, who died in 1886, Verlaine, his emotional distress compounded by a variety of incapacitating physical ills, was to spend his final years in and out of a number of Paris hospitals and increasingly tawdry rooming houses, attended by devoted doctors and supported by a growing coterie of charitable and generous admirers. One of the latter was the young artist F.-A. Cazals, object of Verlaine's unrequited and more-than-platonic attentions, who, despite the poet's unreasonable jealousies, would nonetheless remain a faithful friend, and who would frequently sketch him.

It was during one of his many stays at the Hôpital Broussais that Verlaine completed the collection *Amour,* many of whose poems had been written during the preceding decade under the same religious, almost mystical inspiration as those of *Sagesse,* to which it was originally intended as something of a sequel, along with an element of patriotic fervor and political sarcasm. The volume included in its pages a number of sonnets dedicated to friends and luminaries; among them, the venerable Victor Hugo, poet-theoretician Charles Morice, composer Emmanuel Chabrier, and, in an especially soulful recollection, his former brother-in-law Charles de Sivry. But it seems to have had as its real *raison d'être* the touching twenty-five-poem cycle devoted to Lucien Létinois, some dating from before his death, some from after, and all providing a poignant testimony to Verlaine's affection.

Amour was published by Vanier in 1888. There is an irony, no doubt intentional, in the fact that the entire collection, so much and so important a part of which revolves about Verlaine's "adopted" son—as one of the poems laments: "Puisque l'on m'avait volé mon fils réel" (Since they had stolen my real son from me)—was dedicated, as was its last pathetic poem, to his flesh-and-blood son, Georges, now himself an adolescent too, lost to him through estrangement as was the young Lucien through death.

❊

"Ta voix grave et basse…"

Ta voix grave et basse
Pourtant était douce
Comme du velours,
Telle, en ton discours,
Sur de sombre mousse
De belle eau qui passe.

Ton rire éclatait
Sans gêne et sans art,
Franc, sonore et libre,
Tel, au bois qui vibre,
Un oiseau qui part
Trillant son motet.

Cette voix, ce rire
Font dans ma mémoire
Qui te voit souvent
Et mort et vivant,
Comme un bruit de gloire
Dans quelque martyre.

Ma tristesse en toi
S'égaie à ces sons
Qui disent: "Courage!"
Au cœur que l'orage
Emplit des frissons
De quel triste émoi!

"Your voice was deep and low..."

Your voice was deep and low,
But sweet and soft no less,
Like water, as it passes
Over dark mossy grasses,
In velvet somberness
And hushed pianissimo.

Your laughter would break free—
Artless, untrammeled—ring
Sonorous as the sound
When echoing woods resound
To a bird on the wing
Trilling its melody.

That voice, that laughter, come
Back to my memory, where
I see you—living, dead—
And hear the trumpeted
Sounds, like the glorious blare
Of some soul's martyrdom.

My heart, though sad and aching,
Cheers when it hears those sounds
That say: "Be brave!"; heart filled
With grief, and tempest-chilled;
Heart that the storm confounds
And batters unto breaking.

Orage, ta rage,
Tais-la, que je cause
Avec mon ami
Qui semble endormi,
Mais qui se repose
En un conseil sage...

Storm, calm your agitation;
Let me, in peaceful wise,
Have me a tête-à-tête
With this, my friend, who yet
Appears asleep, but lies
In quiet contemplation…

LUCIEN LÉTINOIS, XXIV

À Georges Verlaine

Ce livre ira vers toi comme celui d'Ovide
    S'en alla vers la Ville.
Il fut chassé de Rome; un coup bien plus perfide
    Loin de mon fils m'exile.

Te reverrai-je? Et quel? Mais quoi! moi mort ou non,
    Voici mon testament:
Crains Dieu, ne hais personne, et porte bien ton nom
    Qui fut porté dûment.

For Georges Verlaine

This book will reach you as, in bygone time,
      Ovid's reached Rome, whence one
Had banished him; an even baser crime
      Exiles me from my son.

For you, this legacy, whether I die
      Or live, or see you more:
Fear God, hate none, bear well your name that I,
      In proper fashion, bore.

Parallèlement (1889)

*D*espite a good many diverse works, biographically signif-
icant and artistically compelling, that were to stem from
his few remaining years of a life divided between hospital
and hovel, *Parallèlement* is generally acknowledged to be Ver-
laine's last major collection. Like *Jadis et naguère*, it is an
assemblage of poems past and present, not only placed in a
temporal parallelism like those of its predecessor, but also
representing the secular current running parallel to the reli-
giosity, in greater or lesser dose, of *Sagesse, Amour,* and
the projected volume *Bonheur* (Happiness). In his
brief preface to the first edition, published by
Vanier in 1889, Verlaine, punning on his title,
as both title and adverb, alluded succinctly to
that intent: "*Parallèlement* à *Sagesse, Amour,*
et aussi à *Bonheur* qui va suivre et conclure"
(*In Parallel* to *Sagesse, Amour,* and also to
Bonheur, which will follow and conclude).
That being the case, one is not surprised to
find here poems of a lusty, earthy, even erot-
ic inspiration: the six Lesbian sonnets origi-
nally published in 1867 in *Les Amies,* and
apparently no longer felt too scandalous for
public consumption; another half-dozen in a
grouping entitled *Filles* (Girls), praising the
corporeal charms of females known and
unknown to Verlaine biographers; the seven

brief poems of *Révérence parler* (With All Due Respect), dating from his confinement in Belgium, and taken from the dismantled collection *Cellulairement;* and the two dozen poems of the cycle *Lunes* (Moons).

It is the latter, in their variety of forms, meters, and rhyme schemes, that are perhaps the most striking of the volume. In several of them Verlaine expresses the desperate cynicism born of his painful, declining days not in eroticism but in a semi-parodic, semi-nostalgic self-deflating mimicry of the characteristic style of his early work. His frankly erotic vein was, however, far from exhausted. Two collections, *Femmes* (Women) and *Hombres* (Men)—the latter's Spanish title being perhaps an echo of his pseudonym manufactured for *Les Amies*—were to appear in 1891 and, posthumously, 1903, respectively, privately printed and not for public sale; the first published by Vanier, the second by A. Messein, and both unbridled in their appeal to the prurient.

❊

Allégorie

Un très vieux temple antique s'écroulant
Sur le sommet indécis d'un mont jaune,
Ainsi qu'un roi déchu pleurant son trône,
Se mire, pâle, au tain d'un fleuve lent.

Grâce endormie et regard somnolent,
Une naïade âgée, auprès d'un aulne,
Avec un brin de saule agace un faune,
Qui lui sourit, bucolique et galant.

Sujet naïf et fade qui m'attristes,
Dis, quel poète entre tous les artistes,
Quel ouvrier morose t'opéra,

Tapisserie usée et surannée,
Banale comme un décor d'opéra,
Factice, hélas! comme ma destinée?

Allegory

A mountain summit—yellow, faint: and there,
An ancient temple-ruin through the haze,
Reflected in a stream's pale, torpid glaze,
Like king dethroned, weeping his lone despair.

Creature of languorous grace and slumberous air,
An aging naiad, by an alder, plays
The tease, twitting, tickling with willow sprays
A smiling satyr—rustic, debonair.

You artless scene, banal cliché; how sad
You make me! Tell me, what dull artist had
The need—what poet dour!—to craft you thus,

You ancient, time-worn, threadbare tapestry,
Décor for some poor opera, spurious,
Counterfeit as my very destiny?

Printemps

Tendre, la jeune femme rousse,
Que tant d'innocence émoustille,
Dit à la blonde jeune fille
Ces mots, tout bas, d'une voix douce:

"Sève qui monte et fleur qui pousse,
Ton enfance est une charmille:
Laisse errer mes doigts dans la mousse
Où le bouton de rose brille,

"Laisse-moi, parmi l'herbe claire,
Boire les gouttes de rosée
Dont la fleur tendre est arrosée,—

"Afin que le plaisir, ma chère,
Illumine ton front candide
Comme l'aube l'azur timide."

LES AMIES, IV

Spring

The woman, young, red-haired of head,
Piqued by the fair and innocent
Blonde maiden, oh so gently bent
Over her and, in whispers, said:

"Blooms yet unplucked, sap yet unspent…
Your childhood is a flower bed:
Let me caress the opulent
Mosses where glows the rosebud red;

"Let me, among the grasses bright,
Sip of the dew that daybreak's hour
Bestrews about the tender flower—

"So that, dear child, bliss and delight
Illumine that chaste brow for you,
As dawn's rays the blue heavens do."

LES AMIES, IV

Été

Et l'enfant répondit, pâmée
Sous la fourmillante caresse
De sa pantelante maîtresse:
"Je me meurs, ô ma bien-aimée!

"Je me meurs; ta gorge enflammée
Et lourde me soûle et m'oppresse;
Ta forte chair d'où sort l'ivresse
Est étrangement parfumée;

"Elle a, ta chair, le charme sombre
Des maturités estivales,—
Elle en a l'ambre, elle en a l'ombre;

"Ta voix tonne dans les rafales,
Et ta chevelure sanglante
Fuit brusquement dans la nuit lente."

LES AMIES, V

Summer

And this, the maiden's hushed reply,
Tingling beneath the soft caress
Of her hard-breathing satyress:
"O lover mine! I swoon, I die!

"I die! Your bosoms, burning, lie
Heavy as heady wine. Ah yes,
I swoon! Your flesh, your breasts possess
Rare scents my sense is ravished by;

"Your flesh, dark with the ripe perfection
Of many a fragrant summer, glows:
Amber perfume, somber reflection;

Your voice; the lusty tremolos
Of gusty breezes; and your hair,
Blood-red, blows on the slow night air."

LES AMIES, V

À Mademoiselle ***

Rustique beauté
Qu'on a dans les coins,
Tu sens bon les foins,
La chair et l'été.

Tes trente-deux dents
De jeune animal
Ne vont point trop mal
À tes yeux ardents.

Ton corps dépravant
Sous tes habits courts,
—Retroussés et lourds,
Tes seins en avant,

Tes mollets farauds,
Ton buste tentant,
—Gai, comme impudent,
Ton cul ferme et gros,

Nous boutent au sang
Un feu bête et doux
Qui nous rend tout fous,
Croupe, rein et flanc.

For Mademoiselle ***

Rustic belle, indiscreet,
Dark-corner *débauchée*,
You smell of new-mown hay,
Of flesh, and summer heat.

Your teeth (all thirty-two)
Like some young beast's, go well
With flashing eyes that tell
Their passion, as yours do.

Your body, scant bedecked,
Beckoning us to sin;
Breasts bulging in their skin,
Your nipples, taut, erect:

Bewitching bust; your calves,
Shameless; your impudent
Young rump, pert, corpulent,
And firmly plump (both halves);

All pump a sweet, daft fire
Into our veins, exciting
Croup, flank (and such), igniting
Our being with mad desire.

Le petit vacher
Tout fier de son cas,
Le maître et ses gas,
Les gas du berger,

Je meurs si je mens,
Je les trouve heureux.
Tous ces culs-terreux,
D'être tes amants.

FILLES, V

The boorish cowherd proud,
Puffed up in his opinions,
The master and his minions,
The shepherd's bumpkin crowd...

Yes, cross my heart, it's true,
I swear by all the gods:
I envy all those clods
Who get to lie with you.

FILLES, V

Impression fausse

Dame souris trotte,
Noire dans le gris du soir,
Dame souris trotte
Grise dans le noir.

On sonne la cloche,
Dormez, les bons prisonniers!
On sonne la cloche:
Faut que vous dormiez.

Pas de mauvais rêve,
Ne pensez qu'à vos amours.
Pas de mauvais rêve:
Les belles toujours!

Le grand clair de lune!
On ronfle ferme à côté.
Le grand clair de lune
En réalité!

Un nuage passe,
Il fait noir comme en un four.
Un nuage passe.
Tiens, le petit jour!

False Impression

Madam mouse trips by,
Black in the dusk's gray light,
Madam mouse trips by,
Gray in the black night.

Now the bell is ringing:
Sleep, lads; locked the keep.
Now the bell is ringing:
You must go to sleep.

Dream no dreadful dreams,
Muse on your damosels,
Dream no dreadful dreams:
Only of your belles!

Brightly shines the moon!
Next door, snores rumble, rife.
Brightly shines the moon
On the facts of life!

Dark, a cloud goes passing,
My cell turns black as coal,
Dark, a cloud goes passing.
Daybreak, bless my soul!

Dame souris trotte,
Rose dans les rayons bleus.
Dame souris trotte:
Debout, paresseux!

R É V É R E N C E   P A R L E R ,   I I

Madam mouse trips by,
Pink in the dawning blue,
Madam mouse trips by.
Up, you dawdler, you!

R É V É R E N C E   P A R L E R ,   I I

Autre

La cour se fleurit de souci
    Comme le front
    De tous ceux-ci
    Qui vont en rond
En flageolant sur leur fémur
    Débilité
    Le long du mur
    Fou de clarté.

Tournez, Samsons sans Dalila,
    Sans Philistin,
    Tournez bien la
    Meule au destin.
Vaincu risible de la loi,
    Mouds tour à tour
    Ton cœur, ta foi
    Et ton amour!

Ils vont! et leurs pauvres souliers
    Font un bruit sec,
    Humiliés,
    La pipe au bec.
Pas un mot ou bien le cachot
    Pas un soupir,
    Il fait si chaud
    Qu'on croit mourir.

Other

The jail yard: marigolds, like woes,
    Mirror the gaze,
    Bedimmed, of those
    Who spend their days—
Round, round—on flagging limbs, despairing,
    Walled in, undone
    By dazzling, glaring,
    Maddening sun.

Poor Samsons, Philistine-deprived—
    Delilah-less,
    Unmanned, unwived—
    In your duress,
Turn, turn fate's mill! And you, law's droll,
    Dumb prey, grind on,
    Till heart, and soul,
    And love are gone!

Chewing their pipes, they come and go,
    With click and clack
    Of their *sabots*,
    Now up, now back…
But not a word or it's the cells!
    No sigh, no breath,
    Or roast in Hell's
    Infernal death.

J'en suis de ce cirque effaré,
    Soumis d'ailleurs
    Et préparé
    À tous malheurs.
Et pourquoi si j'ai contristé
    Ton vœu têtu,
    Société,
    Me choierais-tu?

Allons, frères, bons vieux voleurs,
    Doux vagabonds,
    Filous en fleurs,
    Mes chers, mes bons,
Fumons philosophiquement,
    Promenons-nous
    Paisiblement:
    Rien faire est doux.

RÉVÉRENCE PARLER, III

Part of this fear-bound circus, I
  Have bent my will
  To bear thereby
  My every ill.
For, tell me, world affronted, why
  Should you spare me
  When I defy
  Your firm decree?

Come, brother blackguards, thieves, let's smoke,
  Philosophize...
  Good felon folk,
  Let's temporize
And take a stroll—tramps, thugs in flower—
  In peace a-plenty,
  Relishing our
  Dolce far niente.

RÉVÉRENCE PARLER, III

Tantalized

L'aile où je suis donnant juste sur une gare,
J'entends de nuit (mes nuits sont blanches) la bagarre
Des machines qu'on chauffe et des trains ajustés,
Et vraiment c'est des bruits de nids répercutés
À des dieux de fonte et de verre et gras de houille.
Vous n'imaginez pas comme cela gazouille
Et comme l'on dirait des efforts d'oiselets
Vers des vols tout prochains à des cieux violets
Encore et que le point du jour éclaire à peine.
Ô ces wagons qui vont dévaler dans la plaine!

RÉVÉRENCE PARLER, V

Tantalized

The prison wing that I am quartered in
Faces a railroad station, and the din
Of the machinery, the coupling trains,
Lull my long nights—sleepless for all my pains:
Clattering nests for gods of coal, glass, steel…
My mind fancies young birds that chatter, squeal,
Ready to take their flight, untrammeled; fly
Up, up into the still dark, dawn-tinged sky
Above the plains' deep mauve obscurity.
O trains that can go rolling, rolling free!

R É V É R E N C E   P A R L E R ,   V

Le Dernier Dizain

Ô Belgique qui m'as valu ce dur loisir,
Merci! J'ai pu du moins réfléchir et saisir
Dans le silence doux et blanc de tes cellules
Les raisons qui fuyaient comme des libellules
À travers les roseaux bavards d'un monde vain,
Les raisons de mon être éternel et divin,
Et les étiqueter comme en un beau musée
Dans les cases en fin cristal de ma pensée.
Mais, ô Belgique, assez de ce huis-clos têtu!
Ouvre enfin, car c'est bon pour une fois, sais-tu!

BRUXELLES, AOÛT 1873 - MONS,
JANVIER 1875. / RÉVÉRENCE PARLER, VII

The Last Stanza

Belgium, whom I owe my harsh leisure to,
My thanks! At least I have, because of you,
Pondered in white-walled peace, and caught the whys
And hows—that tried to flee, like dragonflies
Flitting mid life's vain-muttering reeds—of my
Eternal heavenly life, newfound, that I
Mounted and labeled, each one neatly placed,
Set in my mind's museum, crystal-cased.
But Belgium, it's enough! Don't you agree?
Open your stolid prison: let me be!

BRUSSELS, AUGUST 1873 - MONS,
JANUARY 1875. / RÉVÉRENCE PARLER, VII

À la manière de Paul Verlaine

C'est à cause du clair de la lune
Que j'assume ce masque nocturne
Et de Saturne penchant son urne
Et de ces lunes l'une après l'une.

Des romances sans paroles ont,
D'un accord discord ensemble et frais,
Agacé ce cœur fadasse exprès,
Ô le son, le frisson qu'elles ont!

Il n'est pas que vous n'ayez fait grâce
À quelqu'un qui vous jetait l'offense:
Or, moi, je pardonne à mon enfance
Revenant fardée et non sans grâce.

Je pardonne à ce mensonge-là
En faveur en somme du plaisir
Très banal drôlement qu'un loisir
Douloureux un peu m'inocula.

LUNES, II

In the Style of Paul Verlaine

It's the moonlight's fault if I put on
My night-mask; Saturn's fault, too, it is—
Pouring from that gloomy urn of his—
And those moons' too: moons, moons, on and on...

Songs without words, that together sound
Cool, discordant chords, eager to smart
This insipid, dull, lackluster heart,
O the chill, the shudder in their sound!

No, it's not as if you've not made up
With the one who vexed you: unconcerned,
I forgive my childhood, now returned,
Face still pert, though rather much made up.

I forgive that lie I lived—ah me!—
For the well-worn pleasure, tedious,
Droll, with which my leisure, ponderous,
Not without its pains, injected me.

LUNES, II

Limbes

L'imagination, reine,
Tient ses ailes étendues,
Mais la robe qu'elle traîne
A des lourdeurs éperdues.

Cependant que la Pensée,
Papillon, s'envole et vole,
Rose et noir clair, élancée
Hors de la tête frivole.

L'imagination, sise
En son trône, ce fier siège!
Assiste, comme indécise,
À tout ce preste manège,

Et le papillon fait rage,
Monte et descend, plane et vire:
On dirait dans un naufrage
Des culbutes du navire.

La reine pleure de joie
Et de peine encore, à cause
De son cœur qu'un chaud pleur noie,
Et n'entend goutte à la chose.

Limbo

Queen Imagination—she
Of the outspread wings: her gown
Royal, trailing regally,
Hanging heavy, weighs her down.

Meanwhile, Thought, mere butterfly—
Flash of pink and black—takes flight,
Bids capricious head good-bye,
Flits, flies, to her heart's delight.

And Imagination, sitting
On her grand throne, watches all
That adroit, deft flying, flitting,
Not quite sure what may befall,

As our butterfly—right, left,
Up, down, forth, back—rides the breeze
Like a sailboat, helm-bereft,
Bobbing on the gale-racked seas.

And the queen weeps, both in pain
And in joy, though she has no
Notion—none!—how to explain
Why her heart wails, whimpers so.

Psyché Deux pourtant se lasse.
Son vol est la main plus lente
Que cent tours de passe-passe
Ont faite toute tremblante.

Hélas, voici l'agonie!
Qui s'en fût formé l'idée?
Et tandis que, bon génie
Plein d'une douceur lactée,

La bestiole céleste
S'en vient palpiter à terre,
La Folle-du-Logis reste
Dans sa gloire solitaire!

LUNES, V

But soon Psyche's incarnation
Tires: her flight is like a hand
Skilled in prestidigitation,
Doing more sleights than it had planned,

Quivering now in agony!
Ah, who could have, in his blindness,
Guessed the fell catastrophe:
Sprite filled with the milk of kindness—

Sky's mite—falls to earth, remains
Gasping, dying... End of story:
Now Queen Madgination reigns
Solitary in her glory.

LUNES, V

Lombes

Deux femmes des mieux m'ont apparu cette nuit.
Mon rêve était au bal, je vous demande un peu!
L'une d'entre elles maigre assez, blonde, un œil bleu,
Un noir et ce regard mécréant qui poursuit.

L'autre, brune au regard sournois qui flatte et nuit,
Seins joyeux d'être vus, dignes d'un demi-dieu!
Et toutes deux avaient, pour rappeler le jeu
De la main chaude, sous la traîne qui bruit,

Des bas de dos très beaux et d'une gaîté folle
Auxquels il ne manquait vraiment que la parole,
Royale arrière-garde aux combats du plaisir.

Et ces Dames—scrutez l'armorial de France—
S'efforçaient d'entamer l'orgueil de mon désir,
Et n'en revenaient pas de mon indifférence.

VOUZIERS (ARDENNES),
13 AVRIL - 23 MAI 1885. / LUNES, VI

Loins

Last night two women came to me, a pair
Fairer than fair. (Imagine! In my dream
My thought was of the ball, strange though it seem!)
One, with a darkness-fraught, menacing glare—

One eye, black, one of blue; thin, blonde of hair.
The other, with a look that seemed to scheme
And flatter: hair, brown; breasts, divine, supreme!
Both lovelies, rich of loin, with that proud air,

Joyous, that makes the hand, hot, tingle at
Those rustling underskirt delights; loins that
(Lustful rear-guard!) lacked only speech for battle.

And Ladies, they (search France's heraldry!)
Sought to arouse my passion with their prattle,
Astonished at my utter apathy.

VOUZIERS (ARDENNES),

13 APRIL - 23 MAY 1885. / LUNES, VI

◁ 177 ▷

La Dernière Fête Galante

Pour une bonne fois séparons-nous,
Très chers messieurs et si belles mesdames.
Assez comme cela d'épithalames,
Et puis là, nos plaisirs furent trop doux.

Nul remords, nul regret vrai, nul désastre!
C'est effrayant ce que nous nous sentons
D'affinités avecque les moutons
Enrubannés du pire poétastre.

Nous fûmes trop ridicules un peu
Avec nos airs de n'y toucher qu'à peine.
Le Dieu d'amour veut qu'on ait de l'haleine,
Il a raison! Et c'est un jeune Dieu.

Séparons-nous, je vous le dis encore.
Ô que nos cœurs qui furent trop bêlants,
Dès ce jourd'hui réclament, trop hurlants,
L'embarquement pour Sodome et Gomorrhe!

LUNES

The Last "Fête Galante"

Once and for all, enough! Let's bid adieu,
Gentlemen oh so fine, belles oh so fair.
An end to nuptial pleasures, pair by pair;
So cloying sweet were they, *merci beaucoup!*

No, no remorse, regrets, disasters: so it
Goes. Oh, how frightful, when we think that we
Shared the cliché—that vain affinity
For sheep (beribboned!)—of the pseudo-poet!

Oh, how absurd we were, dainty, polite
Unto a fault, loath to be energetic:
The God of love wants life in our aesthetic—
A young God, virile, vigorous… and right.

And so let's bid adieu. Off with the flora,
Fauna of our soft-blurting, bleating heart,
That yearns, this day, transfigured, to depart
With howl and hoot, for Sodom and Gomorrah.

LUNES

FROM

Dédicaces (1890)

*B*ecause of a falling-out with publisher Vanier, the first
edition of *Dédicaces*, with a portrait of Verlaine by
Cazals, one of its prominent dedicatees, was pub-
lished by subscription under the aegis of the
review *La Plume,* whose literary soirées the
poet had begun to frequent when health and
increasingly frequent and promiscuous
homo- and heterosexual adventures permit-
ted. (Among the last-mentioned were his
questionable liaisons with his late-life
companions and muses Eugénie
Krantz and Philomène Boudin.)
That edition, appearing in 1890,
contained only forty-one poems, son-
nets for the most part, dedicated, as the preface
announced, to a variety of poet-friends and other artists,
well-known and lesser-known: "quelques amis et bons cama-
rades de l'auteur qui les leur *dédie* exclusivement sans autre
intention que de leur plaire" (a few friends and good com-
rades of the author, who *dedicates* them exclusively to them,
with no intention other than to please them). Verlaine, in the
same brief preface, excused himself for any significant omis-
sions, blaming them on the intentionally slim dimensions of
the volume.

A goodly number of those omissions were remedied
when, he and Vanier having reconciled their differences, the

latter published a second edition in 1894, with many new poems, more than doubling the size of the first. Considerably more varied in form, these additions were dedicated not only to the well-known and the lesser-known—the likes of Rimbaud, Verlaine's close friend and biographer Edmond Lepelletier, the picturesque Bibi-Purée, et al.—but even, in several instances, the unknown; passing acquaintances, more than likely, concealed behind poem titles of conventional anonymity.

While the craftsmanship of these *hommages* is generally (but not always) beyond technical reproach, revealing a Verlaine still adventuresome in matters of form, meter, and rhyme, most critics agree that, as occasional verse brought to life for reasons less than purely aesthetic, they provided Verlaine with an excuse for continuing a creativity already, sadly, beginning to lack the fire of inner conviction.

✳

Souvenir de Manchester

À Theodore C. London

Je n'ai vu Manchester que d'un coin de Salford,
Donc très mal et très peu, quel que fût mon effort
À travers le brouillard et les courses pénibles
Au possible, en dépit d'hansoms inaccessibles
Presque, grâce à ma jambe male et mes pieds bots.
N'importe, j'ai gardé des souvenirs plus beaux
De cette ville que l'on dit industrielle,—
Encore que de telle ô qu'intellectuelle
Place où ma vanité devait se pavaner
Soi-disant mieux—et dussiez-vous vous étonner
Des semblantes naïvetés de cette épître,
Ô vous! quand je parlais du haut de mon pupitre
Dans cette salle où l' "élite" de Manchester
Applaudissait en Verlaine l'auteur d'*Esther*,
Et que je proclamais, insoucieux du pire
Ou du meilleur, mon culte énorme pour Shakspeare.

30 JANVIER 1894. / LVIII

Recollection of Manchester

For Theodore C. London

A glimpse of Salford, just a corner, was
All that I saw of Manchester, because,
Thanks to the fog and to my clubfoot gait—
And hansom cabs that circumambulate
Everywhere else, it seems!—my efforts were
Sincere but vain; and so no connoisseur
Of Manchester am I. And yet, no matter:
Priggishly though the rest of you might natter,
Decry its factories, its industries,
Telling me how much more some towns would please
My intellectual's vanities! still, sweet
The memories of that Manchester "elite,"
There, in that hall—naïve, no doubt, as when
They praised Racine, taking him for Verlaine!—
As I proclaimed, for better or for worse,
My utter reverence for Shakespeare's verse.

30 JANUARY 1894. / LVIII

À Edmond Lepelletier

Mon plus vieil ami survivant
D'un groupe déjà de fantômes
Qui dansent comme des atomes
Dans un rais de lune devant

Nos yeux assombris et rêvant
Sous les ramures polychromes
Que l'automne arrondit en dômes
Funèbres où gémit le vent,

Bah! la vie est si courte en somme
—Quel sot réveil après quel somme!—
Qu'il ne faut plus penser aux morts

Que pour les plaindre et pour les oindre
De regrets exempts de remords,
Car n'allons-nous pas les rejoindre?

L X

For Edmond Lepelletier

My oldest friend, last of that score
(And more) gone on to their reward,
That dear departed phantom horde
Dancing like moonbeam specks before

Our dimmed eyes, musing evermore
Beneath the autumn's grim concord
Of colors, dour bough-domed greensward,
Where moans and wails the wind, heartsore…

Bah! Life's too short for us to keep
Mourning the dead—life: between sleep
Of birth and death, that meager waking!—

Except to salve them in their slumber
With pity—no remorse, no aching
Heart; for won't we, too, join their number?

L X

À Arthur Rimbaud

Mortel, ange ET démon, autant dire Rimbaud,
Tu mérites la prime place en ce mien livre,
Bien que tel sot grimaud t'ait traité de ribaud
Imberbe et de monstre en herbe et de potache ivre.

Les spirales d'encens et les accords de luth
Signalent ton entrée au temple de mémoire
Et ton nom radieux chantera dans la gloire,
Parce que tu m'aimas ainsi qu'il le fallut.

Les femmes te verront grand jeune homme très fort,
Très beau d'une beauté paysanne et rusée,
Très désirable, d'une indolence qu'osée!

L'histoire t'a sculpté triomphant de la mort
Et jusqu'aux purs excès jouissant de la vie,
Tes pieds blancs posés sur la tête de l'Envie!

L X I I

For Arthur Rimbaud

Human, an angel, AND a demon—or,
In other words, Rimbaud! Here are you placed
In honor, though twits fancied you a whore
Smooth-faced, a budding fiend; drunk pup, disgraced.

The lute twangs and the incense twirls, entwined
In memory's temple, where, forever bright,
Your name will sing, in radiant light enshrined,
Because you loved me, and to love was right.

Women will see you young and vigorous,
Charming in all your slyly peasant beauty:
Rogue given more to dalliance than to duty!

Pose death-defying: history sculpts you thus,
Reveling, on life's pure excesses fed,
White feet, in triumph, poised on Envy's head.

L X I I

À Bibi-Purée

Bibi-Purée
Type épatant
Et drôle tant!

Quel Dieu te crée
Ce chic, pourtant,
Qui nous agrée,

Pourtant, aussi,
Ta gentillesse
Notre liesse,
Et ton souci

De l'obligeance,
Notre gaîté,
Ta pauvreté,
Ton opulence?

L X X X V I

For Bibi-Purée

Curious bird,
Bibi-Purée,
Droll popinjay!

What God conferred
On you that air
Gay, debonair,

And with it, too,
Your kindness, our
Delight, your power
To please, to do

Our pleasure—whence
Our levity—
Your paupery,
Your opulence?

L X X X V I

Bonheur (1891)

*W*hen the collection *Bonheur* (Happiness) was eventual-
ly brought out by Vanier in the spring of 1891,
though originally promised to another Paris publisher during
his and Verlaine's squabble, it had already been in the making
for several years. Long projected as the third "panel" of the
triptych *Sagesse-Amour-Bonheur,* many of its thirty-three
poems dated from as early as 1887; some, indeed, were writ-
ten during yet another hospital stay and while taking a doc-
tor-imposed "cure" at Aix-les-Bains.

Intended for a time to bear the more appropriate title
Espoir (Hope), its definitive title is an ironic commentary—
perhaps a bit of sympathetic magic meant to badger the
gods?—on Verlaine's continuous quest for contentment, be it
in his more and more degrading sexual encounters with
sundry partners, in his almost desperate, quasi-mystical
bouts with religiosity, or even in the artistic camaraderie of a
literary world beginning once again to ignore him as a poet
of the present, no longer the darling of the Décadents, while
continuing to respect him as a poet of the past.

Aesthetically, it was Verlaine's stated desire, in these
poems, to write what he characterized as a *poésie dure* (hard
poetry), no doubt in accordance with the rigorously conserv-
ative and conventional tenets of the so-called École Romane
(Roman School) of Jean Moréas, with which Verlaine flirted
for a while, perhaps less from poetic conviction than from a
need for artistic fellowship to counter his growing isolation.

While one might not want to go so far as to share the uncharitable opinion of some that the poems in *Bonheur* are Verlaine's dullest, it is hard not to accept the judgment of most that, dogmatic and preachy, they are certainly inferior to those of *Sagesse* and *Amour,* noble intentions notwithstanding. Surely they have none of the grace, none of the fluidity and charm of his early works, on the one hand, nor, on the other, any of the flippancy of manner or daring metrical and rhyming innovation that some of his later works were yet to display. Only occasionally—notably in the final poem, from 1888, translated here—does he rise above the ponderous turgidity of the collection as a whole.

※

"Voix de Gabriel…"

Voix de Gabriel
Chez l'humble Marie,
Cloches de Noël
Dans la nuit fleurie,
Siècles, célébrez
Mes sens délivrés.

Martyrs, troupe blanche,
Et les confesseurs,
Fruits d'or de la branche,
Vous, frères et sœurs,
Vierges dans la gloire,
Chantez ma victoire.

Les Saints ignorés,
Vertus qu'on méprise,
Qui nous sauverez
Par votre entremise,
Priez, que la foi
Demeure humble en moi.

Pécheurs, par le monde,
Qui vous repentez
Dans l'ardeur profonde
D'être rachetés,
Or je vous contemple,
Donnez-moi l'exemple.

"In Mary's humble ear…"

In Mary's humble ear
The angel Gabriel's voice;
The Yule bells ringing clear
In flowering night: rejoice,
You generations, sing
My mind's delivering.

Martyrs, confessors, all
Your spotless retinue,
Boughs' golden fruit! I call
My brothers, sisters, you
Of blessèd charity,
To hail my victory.

Virtues despised and Saints
Ignored, whose intercession
Will cleanse our sins, our taints,
And lead us from transgression,
Pray that my faith remain
Free of all pride profane.

Yes, sinners everywhere,
Who fervently repent
And yearn, with every prayer,
Contrite and penitent,
To earn redress, I pray
You show my soul the way.

Nature, animaux,
Eaux, plantes et pierres,
Vos simples travaux
Sont d'humbles prières.
Vous obéissez:
Pour Dieu, c'est assez.

X X X I I I

God's are the beasts, and His,
You plants, rocks, rivers too;
All your existence is
A humble prayer; you do
His every wish and whim:
And that's enough for Him.

Chansons pour Elle (1891)

*W*ith no hope for Verlaine that the young Cazals would return his affections in the desired manner, Eugénie Krantz and Philomène Boudin, seedy paramours of his declining days, were to dominate the rest of his ambivalent sentimental and sexual life. They would dominate as well much of his remaining poetic production. Three of his next

four brief collections were directly inspired by either or both. Though not wholly disinterested in their relations with him—Eugénie especially took advantage, for a time, of what meager material resources he had not yet drunk away—they did nonetheless remain faithful friends if not always faithful lovers.

The *Elle* in the title of the slim volume *Chansons pour Elle* (Songs for Her), published by Vanier at the end of 1891, was, according to most sources, almost exclusively Eugénie, whom Verlaine had met during the spring of that year. Composed in a breezy, even impromptu-appearing style, its two dozen short poems recall the diversity of meters and rhymes of the "early Verlaine," though with none of the grace or depth of emotion. A far cry from the romantic effusions of *La Bonne Chanson*, for example, and glorifying the strictly sensual—indeed, the blatantly animalistic—rather than the sentimental, they reveal a poet become brashly defiant in his acceptance of his powerlessness to resist the degradations of the flesh; at least, that is, until the final line of the last poem of the collection, where he laments his lost faith: "Ô le temps béni quand j'étais ce mystique" (O the blessèd time when I that mystic was!).

Earthy and banal though most of them surely are, the poems of *Chansons pour Elle*, contrasting sharply with the liturgical tone of *Bonheur*, offer the reader a frivolous relief from Verlaine's far more profound, but tedious, outpourings.

✳

"Or, malgré ta cruauté…"

Or, malgré ta cruauté
Affectée, et l'air très faux
De sale méchanceté
Dont, bête, tu te prévaux,

J'aime ta lasciveté !

Et quoiqu'en dépit de tout
Le trop factice dégoût
Que me dicte ton souris
Qui m'est, à mes dams et coût,

Rouge aux crocs blancs de souris !

Je t'aime comme l'on croit,
Et mon désir fou qui croît,
Tel un champignon des prés,
S'érige ainsi que le Doigt

D'un Terme là tout exprès.

"*Yes, despite your cruel excess...*"

Yes, despite your cruel excess,
Put on just for show; despite
Your false air of evil; yes,
That false air you relish, quite,

Still I love your lustfulness.

And, my love, in spite of all
My own well-feigned show of gall
At your grin—deep crimson-lipped,
For my hurt and harm withal—

Mousy grin: white fangs, sharp-tipped!

Still I love you, don't you know!
And my passion seems to grow
Mushroom-like, erect, unbending
As a Finger, waggling "No!"

Signaling the End impending.

Donc, malgré ma cruauté
Affectée, et l'air très faux
De pire méchanceté,
Dont, bête, je me prévaux,

Aime ma simplicité.

I V

So, despite my cruel excess,
Put on just for show; despite
My worse air of evil; yes,
That false air I relish, quite,

Love me for my artlessness.

I V

"Je suis plus pauvre que jamais…"

Je suis plus pauvre que jamais
    Et que personne;
Mais j'ai ton cou gras, tes bras frais,
    Ta façon bonne
De faire l'amour, et le tour
    Leste et frivole
Et la caresse, nuit et jour,
    De ta parole.

Je suis riche de tes beaux yeux,
    De ta poitrine,
Nid follement voluptueux,
    Couche ivoirine
Où mon désir, las d'autre part,
    Se ravigore
Et pour d'autres ébats repart
    Plus brave encore…

Sans doute tu ne m'aimes pas
    Comme je t'aime,
Je sais combien tu me trompas
    Jusqu'à l'extrême.
Que me fait puisque je ne vis
    Qu'en ton essence,
Et que tu tiens mes sens ravis
    Sous ta puissance?

V I I

"I'm poorer than I've ever been…"

I'm poorer than I've ever been,
    No one has less;
But mine, your plump neck, arms' cool skin;
    And mine—ah yes!—
The lovely way you love, and your
    Mischief's delight,
Your words' caresses, *mon amour,*
    By day, by night.

Rich am I with the beauty of
    Your eyes, your breast—
That nest of wild and fleshly love—
    The ivoriest
Of couches, where my lust, worn through,
    Revives, until
It undertakes more derring-do
    Lustier still…

Doubtless you love me less than I
    Love you; I know
How much you've cheated—where, when, why,
    With whom. But so?
What matter, since my life, my all,
    My being unmanned,
My very senses lie in thrall
    To your command?

VII

"Vrai, nous avons trop d'esprit…"

Vrai, nous avons trop d'esprit,
Chérie!
Je crois que mal nous en prit,
Chérie,
D'ainsi lutter corps à corps
Encore,
Sans repos et sans remords
Encore!

Plus, n'est-ce pas? de ces luttes
Sans but,
Plus de ces mauvaises flûtes.
Ce luth,
Ô ce luth de bien se faire
Tel air,
Toujours vibrant, chanson chère
Dans l'air!

Et n'ayons donc plus d'esprit,
T'en prie!
Tu vois que mal nous en prit…
T'en prie.
Soyons bons tout bêtement,
Charmante,
Aimons-nous aimablement,
M'amante!

X I

"True, we don't know when to quit…"

True, we don't know when to quit,
  My sweet!
And you'll see, we've paid for it,
  My sweet,
Up and down, and chin to chin,
  Again,
No regrets, night out, night in,
  Again!

So? No more of those disputes
  Now moot,
Finished too those untuned flutes.
  Ah, lute,
Well-strung lute, yes, let's prefer
  Your air,
Tender, throbbing song, to stir
  The air.

Please, let's say it's time to quit,
  Petite!
See how much we've paid for it…
  Petite,
Let's behave as love inclines,
  Divine,
Let's love simply—no designs—
  Wench mine!

X I

"Es-tu brune ou blonde?..."

Es-tu brune ou blonde?
Sont-ils noirs ou bleus,
Tes yeux?
Je n'en sais rien mais j'aime leur clarté profonde,
Mais j'adore le désordre de tes cheveux.

Es-tu douce ou dure?
Est-il sensible ou moqueur,
Ton cœur?
Je n'en sais rien mais je rends grâce à la nature
D'avoir fait de ton cœur mon maître et mon vainqueur.

Fidèle, infidèle?
Qu'est-ce que ça fait,
Au fait
Puisque toujours dispose à couronner mon zèle
Ta beauté sert de gage à mon plus cher souhait.

X I I I

"Blonde? Brown? Which is your hair?…"

Blonde? Brown? Which is your hair?
Black? Color of the skies,
     Your eyes?
Who knows? But I adore their limpid air
And your hair's jumble, tumbling sloven-wise.

Tender or rough? Which one?
Sweet-soft or bitter-tart,
     Your heart?
Who knows? But I thank nature, next to none,
For making me its subject, with her art.

Faithful? Unfaithful? Which?
What difference, since, indeed,
     You feed
My love, my lust, with beauties that enrich
My pleasure, serve my being's most treasured need!

X I I I

"Tu crois au marc de café…"

Tu crois au marc de café,
    Aux présages, aux grands jeux:
Moi je ne crois qu'en tes grands yeux.

Tu crois aux contes de fées,
    Aux jours néfastes, aux songes,
Moi je ne crois qu'en tes mensonges.

Tu crois en un vague Dieu,
    En quelque saint spécial,
En tel *Ave* contre tel mal.

Je ne crois qu'aux heures bleues
    Et roses que tu m'épanches
Dans la volupté des nuits blanches!

Et si profonde est ma foi
    Envers tout ce que je croi
Que je ne vis plus que pour toi.

x   x

"You believe in superstitions…"

You believe in superstitions,
Coffee grounds to scrutinize:
All I believe in is your eyes.

You believe in premonitions,
Fairy tales, dreams prophesying:
All I believe in is your lying.

You believe in spirit powers,
Vaguely God-like, and some saint
With prayers for this or that complaint.

I believe in pink-blue hours
That you strew about me, through
My wanton, wakeful nights with you!

And so deep my faith, somehow,
That, by everything, I vow
That you are all I live for now.

x x

"Lorsque tu cherches tes puces…"

Lorsque tu cherches tes puces
    C'est très rigolo.
Que de ruses, que d'astuces!
    J'aime ce tableau.
C'est alliciant en diable
    Et mon cœur en bat
D'un battement préalable
    À quelque autre ébat.

Sous la chemise tendue
    Au large, à deux mains,
Tes yeux scrutent l'étendue
    Entre tes durs seins.
Toujours tu reviens bredouille,
    D'ailleurs, de ce jeu.
N'importe, il me trouble et brouille,
    Ton sport, et pas peu!

Lasse-toi d'être défaite
    Aussi sottement.
Viens payer une autre fête
    À ton corps charmant
Qu'une chasse infructueuse
    Par monts et par vaux.
Tu seras victorieuse…
    Si je ne prévaux!

X X I

"Lover, when you look for lice…"

Lover, when you look for lice,
    It's a howling sight.
Every trick, every device,
    Whets my appetite!
And my heart goes pounding in a
    Rhythm diabolic,
Like the one when we begin a
    Different kind of frolic!

Blouse outstretched between your hands,
    Sharp-eyed, you inspect
All the tender space that stands
    'Twixt your teats erect.
Empty-handed, you return
    From your sport; and yet,
You can bet it makes me burn
    In a lusty sweat!

Give up this hullabaloo,
    This frustrating folly:
Come and treat your body to
    Something far more jolly
Than this vain hunt over mound,
    Hill, dale—outer, inner—
You'll prevail… Though, I'll be bound,
    I'll come out the winner!

X X I

"J'ai rêvé de toi cette nuit…"

J'ai rêvé de toi cette nuit:
Tu te pâmais en mille poses
Et roucoulais des tas de choses…

Et moi, comme on savoure un fruit
Je te baisais à bouche pleine
Un peu partout, mont, val ou plaine.

J'étais d'une élasticité,
D'un ressort vraiment admirable:
Tudieu, quelle haleine et quel râble!

Et toi, chère, de ton côté,
Quel râble, quelle haleine, quelle
Élasticité de gazelle…

Au réveil, ce fut, dans tes bras,
Mais plus aiguë et plus parfaite,
Exactement la même fête!

X X I I

"I dreamed of you last night; and you…"

I dreamed of you last night; and you
Swooned in a thousand posturings,
Warbling and cooing a myriad things…

And me, I kissed you through and through,
As one might suck a fruit, all round,
Everywhere—hill, plain, valley, mound.

I was a pliant spring, elastic,
Coiling, uncoiling. Damn! My back,
My gasps… Ah, what a firm attack!

And you, my sweet, no less fantastic:
Your back, your gasps, your bouncings, boundings,
Like a gazelle, spanned the surroundings…

When I awoke to your caress,
The same delights were ours: not less,
But more our festive lustfulness!

X X I I

Liturgies intimes (1892)

*T*he first edition of *Liturgies intimes* was published in March of 1892, on a subscription basis, by the Catholic journal *Le Saint-Graal* (The Holy Grail), directed by Symbolist poet Emmanuel Signoret. The list of subscribers brought together seasoned and youthful Verlaine admirers of many stripes, artistic and even political, from statesman and future president Félix Faure, ill-fated reactionary Charles Maurras, and composer Vincent d'Indy, to such literati as poets Jean Moréas, Henri de Régnier, and the young André Gide. A second, slightly expanded edition was published the following year by Vanier. Between the two editions, Verlaine, continuing to enjoy literary respect if not unalloyed artistic admiration—a respect for his critical opinions and poetic insights more than for his own verse of the moment—periodically left his various hospital beds long enough to accept invitations to deliver several series of lectures in Holland and Belgium, returning to squander his honoraria on the unappreciative Eugénie.

Containing twenty-five short pieces in all, remnants of *Sagesse, Amour,* and especially *Bonheur,* and aimed, as Verlaine himself states in the preface to the first edition, at "un tout petit public d'élite" (a small, select public), *Liturgies intimes* is something of a last gasp of religiosity in his *œuvre,* as well as a last, nostalgic, despairing but ineffectual personal act of faith.

Among the collection's repetition-worn credos, kyries, and glorias, one poem stands out. The curious liminary dedication *"À Charles Baudelaire"*—a sonnet, appropriately enough—was added to the second edition but had apparently been intended originally for inclusion in *Dédicaces.* Calling somewhat into question the genuineness of Baudelaire's Catholicity, Verlaine, who had written an important laudatory article on the poet in 1865, seems to be rejecting, symbolically, in the person of his once-adulated model, the values (or non-values) of his "saturnine" youth. The last poem in the collection closes the circle, summing up in the breast-beatings of a "vil et laid pécheur" (vile and ugly sinner) Verlaine's often-expressed, and by now a trifle hollow-sounding, lamentations.

✳

À Charles Baudelaire

Je ne t'ai pas connu, je ne t'ai pas aimé,
Je ne te connais point et je t'aime encor moins:
Je me chargerais mal de ton nom diffamé,
Et si j'ai quelque droit d'être entre tes témoins,

C'est que, d'abord, et c'est qu'ailleurs, vers les Pieds joints
D'abord par les clous froids, puis par l'élan pâmé
Des femmes de péché—desquelles ô tant oints,
Tant baisés, chrême fol et baiser affamé!—

Tu tombas, tu prias, comme moi, comme toutes
Les âmes que la faim et la soif sur les routes
Poussaient belles d'espoir au Calvaire touché!

—Calvaire juste et vrai, Calvaire où, donc, ces doutes,
Ci, çà, grimaces, art, pleurent de leurs déroutes.
Hein? mourir simplement, nous, hommes de péché.

For Charles Baudelaire

I do not know you now, or like you, nor
Did I first know or like you, I admit.
It's not for me to furbish and restore
Your name: if I take up the cause for it,

It's that we both have known the exquisite
Joys of two feet together pressed: His, or
Our whores'! He, nailed; they, swooning in love's fit,
Madly anointed, kissed, bowed down before!

You fell, you prayed. And so did I, like all
Those souls whom thirst and hunger, yearningly,
Shining with hope, urged on to Calvary!

—Calvary, righteous, where—here, there—our fall,
In art-contorted doubts, weeps its chagrin.
A simple death, eh? we, brothers in sin.

Odes en son honneur (1893)

*I*n the summer of 1893 Verlaine, to the surprise of many,
placed himself in nomination—unsuccessfully—for a
vacant seat in the venerable but stodgy Académie Française.
One might reflect, cynically, that the desire to join that
august body of "immortals" could only be a tacit admission
that his creative glories were a thing of the past. Be that as it
may, despite his numerous and progressively worsening ail-
ments, he was able to complete two successful lecture tours,
one of which took him across the Channel to London, Man-
chester, and Oxford, a tribute at least to the continuing
celebrity of his name. At the same time he persisted in
remaining productive, forcing a poetic vein that, brightened
by only occasional flashes of novelty and flair, had clearly
begun to run dry.

In a pendulum-swing back from the religious to the pro-
fane, two short collections, each published by Vanier in May
of the same year, followed *Liturgies intimes.* It is generally
assumed that both were written for and about Philomène
Boudin. *Élégies,* the first—by a single day—comprises a
dozen classically styled rhymed couplets, as ponderous in the
secular realm as *Bonheur* had been in the devotional. Far
more engaging is the second of the pair, *Odes en son honneur*
(Odes in Her Honor), begun almost immediately after the
publication of *Chansons pour Elle,* devoted to Philomène's
rival, Eugénie Krantz.

According to Verlaine himself, the nineteen *odes* that constitute this collection were intended to be more serious in style than the somewhat bawdy *chansons* composed for Eugénie; similar to them in inspiration, to be sure, but decked out "en faux-col et en Cronstadt" (in high collar and top hat). While their form is, indeed, generally more sober, that alleged seriousness, it must be said, is not always apparent, especially in the several pieces where Verlaine, recalling the *blason*-poems of Renaissance writers, extols and venerates specific parts of his mistress's anatomy. Erotic but certainly not pornographic, they echo, in dim and quite respectable fashion, some of the more blatantly unrestrained verses of his youth.

"Tu fus souvent cruelle…"

Tu fus souvent cruelle,
Même injuste parfois,
Mais que fait, ô ma belle,
Puisqu'en toi seule crois

Et puisque suis ta chose.

Que tu me trompes avec Pierre,
Louis, *et cœtera punctum,*
Le sais, mais, là! n'en ai que faire
Ne suis que l'humble factotum

De ton humeur gaie ou morose.

S'il arrive que tu me battes,
Soufflettes, égratignes, tu
Es le maître dans nos pénates,
Et moi le cocu, le battu,

Suis content et vois tout en rose.

"You've often been unkind…"

You've often been unkind,
Even unreasoning
My sweet, but I don't mind,
Since you're my everything

And since I'm just your toy.

Cheat on me with Pierre, Louis,
Et cetera: I know, but what
Can I do, since I'll always be
The humble servant—nothing but—

Of your moroseness or your joy!

Whether you beat, slap, scratch me, you
Are mistress of my board and bed;
You rule the roost, and my life too,
And I, though beaten, cuckolded,

Know pleasure pure, without alloy.

Et puis dame! j'opine
Qu'à me voir ainsi si
Tien, finiras, divine,
Par m'aimoter ainsi

Qu'on s'attache à sa chose.

But, goddess, I'm damn sure
That, seeing how I admit
To being all yours… Well, you're
Bound to love me a bit,

The way we love a toy.

"Riche ventre qui n'a jamais porté…"

Riche ventre qui n'a jamais porté,
Seins opulents qui n'ont pas allaité,
Bras frais et gras, purs de tout soin servile,

Beau cou qui n'a plié que sous le poids
De lents baisers à tous les chers endroits,
Menton où la paresse se profile,

Bouche éclatante et rouge d'où jamais
Rien n'est sorti que propos que j'aimais,
Oiseux et gais—et quel nid de délices!

Nez retroussé quêtant les seuls parfums
De la santé robuste, yeux plus que bruns
Et moins que noirs, indulgemment complices,

Front peu penseur mais pour cela bien mieux,
Longs cheveux noirs dont le grand flot soyeux
Jusques aux reins lourdement se hasarde,

Croupe superbe éprise de loisir
Sauf aux travaux du suprême plaisir,
Aux gais combats dont c'est l'arrière-garde,

Jambes enfin, vaillantes seulement
Dans le plaisant déduit au bon moment
Serrant mon buste ou ballant vers la nue,

"That firm-fleshed belly that has never borne…"

That firm-fleshed belly that has never borne;
Opulent bosom, breasts unnursed, unworn;
Tender arms, plump, not meant for drudgery;

Fair, slender neck, unbent, except when pressed
Beneath long kisses—placed where they please best!
Chin proudly set in idle dignity;

Lips of bright red that never said a word
But that I loved to hear: trite and absurd,
But gay! And what a nest of pure delights!

Nose upturned, nostrils flaring, sucking down
Perfumes of robust health; eyes more than brown
And less than black, indulgent acolytes;

Brow never lost in thought, but better thus;
Hair black, long, lush and silken, luminous,
Billowing down the back its ins and outs;

Majestic rump, given to leisured pose—
Except when bringing up the rear in those
Combats of ours: ecstatic pleasure-bouts;

And legs, tight, tighter still, till, just before,
Clasped taut about my trunk, a-quiver, or
Flailing the air, the very air above her…

Puis, au repos—cuisses, genoux, mollet,—
Fleurant comme ambre et blanches comme lait:
—Tel le pastel d'après ma femme nue.

X I

Then rest… Resting, those thighs, knees, calves, outspent,
Redolent, milk-white in their amber scent:
—This, the pastel vignette of my nude lover.

X I

"Le Livre posthume" (1893–94)

*I*n 1893 and 1894, years of an intense literary activity quite
belying his physical condition, Verlaine had apparently
intended to give the morbidly prognosticatory title *Le Livre
posthume* (The Posthumous Book) to a collection of forty-five
poems of disparate inspiration, style, and date of composi-
tion. Several of them—including one no doubt meant as a
liminary piece, stating somberly that "Le poète a fini sa
tâche…" (The poet's task is done…)—had already appeared
in various journals, and some would also be earmarked for
inclusion in a collection to be entitled *Varia*.

Le Livre posthume never, in fact, appeared as such, either
after or before Verlaine's death, though many of its poems
and those of the likewise unpublished *Varia* were eventually
included in the two editions of the *Œuvres posthumes*, pub-
lished by Vanier and his successor A. Messein, respectively
in 1903 and 1911.

Seven poems, among them a group of five entitled *Frag-
ments*, originally appeared in print as belonging to the pro-
jected *Le Livre posthume*, and are so grouped in the Le Dan-
tec-Borel edition (*Œuvres poétiques complètes*, pp. 816–22).
Though inspired, like so many of Verlaine's late works, by
his pathetic attachment to Philomène, and addressed to her
with a subdued elegance that probably surpassed her unso-
phisticated understanding, they display neither the eroticism
of the *Odes en son honneur* nor the artificial classical ponder-

ousness of the *Élégies*. On the contrary, they are simple, perhaps a trifle idealized, expressions of gratitude for her affection, flawed though it often was, in the face of an ever more obviously impending death, and darkly colored by his resigned acceptance of it.

✳

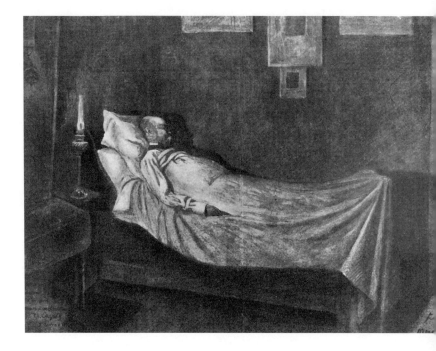

Dernier espoir

Il est un arbre au cimetière
Poussant en pleine liberté,
Non planté par un deuil dicté,—
Qui flotte au long d'une humble pierre.

Sur cet arbre, été comme hiver,
Un oiseau vient qui chante clair
Sa chanson tristement fidèle.
Cet arbre et cet oiseau c'est nous:

Toi le souvenir, moi l'absence
Que le temps—qui passe—recense...
Ah, vivre encore à tes genoux!

Ah, vivre encor! Mais quoi, ma belle,
Le néant est mon froid vainqueur...
Du moins, dis, je vis dans ton cœur?

Last Hope

Beside a humble stone, a tree
Floats in the cemetery's air,
Not planted *in memoriam* there,
But growing wild, uncultured, free.

A bird comes perching there to sing,
Winter and summer, proffering
Its faithful song—sad, bittersweet.
That tree, that bird are you and I:

You, memory; absence, me, that tide
And time record. Ah, by your side
To live again, undying! Aye,

To live again! But *ma petite*,
Now nothingness, cold, owns my flesh…
Will your love keep my memory fresh?

FROM

Épigrammes (1894)

A fourth, very short—and very "chastely" romantic—
collection, *Dans les limbes,* was once more to honor
Philomène, who had been Verlaine's most faithful and solici-
tous visitor "in the limbo" of the Hôpital Broussais through-
out his near-fatal five-month stay in 1893, and would be pub-
lished by Vanier the following year while the ailing poet was
confined yet again.

It was during that latter confinement (this time in the
Hôpital Saint-Louis) that he composed the thirty-
odd heterogeneous pieces of the volume
Épigrammes, many dedicated to promi-
nent and less-than-prominent friends
and acquaintances—the ever-devoted
Cazals among them—and most dis-
playing a now nostalgic, now tongue-
in-cheek personal and artistic self-
awareness.

Apparently written to pass the
time and with no profound aim in
mind, the curious poems of this collec-
tion, published in 1894 by the Bibliothèque
Artistique et Littéraire through the good
offices of the journal *La Plume,* bear Verlaine's assurance, in
three scant prefatory lines, that the little work in question
"fut écrit par un malade qui voulait se distraire et ne pas trop
ennuyer ses contemporains" (was written by a patient who

wanted to amuse himself without overly distressing his contemporaries). The poet concludes this briefest of his prefaces by asking posterity not to take the work too seriously.

"Quand nous irons, si je dois encor la voir…"

Quand nous irons, si je dois encor la voir,
　　Dans l'obscurité du bois noir,

Quand nous serons ivres d'air et de lumière
　　Au bord de la claire rivière,

Quand nous serons d'un moment dépaysés
　　De ce Paris aux cœurs brisés,

Et si la bonté lente de la nature
　　Nous berce d'un rêve qui dure,

Alors, allons dormir du dernier sommeil!
　　Dieu se chargera du réveil.

XIII

"When we go—if I see her yet again…"

When we go—if I see her yet again—
    Off to the shadowed woodland; when

We glut, drunk on the air, beside the gleaming
    Rivulet's glitter, gently streaming;

When, for a while, we leave—in body and mind—
    Paris of broken hearts behind;

And if a kindly nature, leisurely,
    Lulls us in lasting reverie,

Then let us go, our final slumber taking!
    God will be there to work the waking.

X I I I

"Grâce à toi je me vois de dos…"

À F.-A. Cazals

Grâce à toi je me vois de dos
    Et bien plus vraisemblable:
Dans ton croquis, à pas lourdauds,
    Je m'en vais droit au diable.

Moi qui, pour la postérité,
    Sur une aile céleste
Croyais m'envoler, révolté,
    Fatal et tout le reste!

—Je m'achemine doucement,
    D'un trot plus ou moins leste,
Attiré par un double aimant,
    Vers le diable… ou le reste.

X V I I

"It's thanks to you I see how I…"

For F.-A. Cazals

It's thanks to you I see how I
    Look from behind, exactly:
Your drawing shows me lumbering by
    Toward hell, matter-of-factly.

Me, who was sure that I—for all
    My pose rebellious, bestial—
Would fly, after the folderol,
    To afterlife celestial!

—I wend my way to my reward,
    Loping whithersoever,
Drawn by a double magnet toward
    The devil… or whatever.

X V I I

Au bas d'un croquis

(Siège de Paris)

Paul Verlaine (Félix Régamey *pingebat*)
Muet, inattentif aux choses de la rue,
Digère, cependant qu'au lointain on se bat,
Sa ration de lard et son quart de morue.

x x i v

Accompanying a Sketch

(The Siege of Paris)

Verlaine, Paul—artist: Félix Régamey—
Giving the streets' commotion not a nod,
Silent, mid sounds of mayhem and *mêlée*,
Digests his bacon slab and slice of cod.

X X I V

Sur un exemplaire des Fleurs du mal

(Première édition)

Je compare ces vers étranges
Aux étranges vers que ferait
Un marquis de Sade discret
Qui saurait la langue des anges.

XXVIII

On a Copy of *Les Fleurs du mal*

(First Edition)

These poems, strange, are, to my mind,
Like the strange poems that might have sprung
From a Marquis de Sade, refined,
If he could speak the angels' tongue.

X X V I I I

Chair (1896)

*V*erlaine continued his tentative existence for two more
years, aided materially by several government subven-
tions, physically by his devoted doctors, and emotionally by
the attentions of the ever-present Philomène and, especially,
Eugénie. It was at the latter's home, where he had spent the
last few months of his life, that he died, January 8, 1896.

There is a curious irony in the fact that Verlaine wrote
several articles on Rimbaud, the love of his tempestuous
youth (dead some five years before), as well as the preface to
Vanier's edition of the latter's *Poésies complètes,* while living
en ménage, and relatively at peace, with one of the loves of his
waning years, thus summing up, on the eve of his demise,
the enigma and contradiction of his sentimental existence.

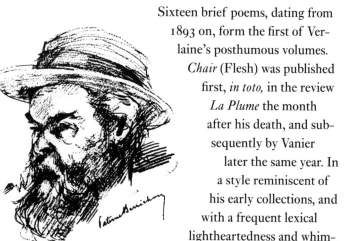

Sixteen brief poems, dating from
1893 on, form the first of Ver-
laine's posthumous volumes.
Chair (Flesh) was published
first, *in toto,* in the review
La Plume the month
after his death, and sub-
sequently by Vanier
later the same year. In
a style reminiscent of
his early collections, and
with a frequent lexical
lightheartedness and whim-

sicality of form clearly at odds with the conditions of their composition, they sing—for Eugénie, Philomène, and perhaps others—the joys of the flesh, but with none of his more recent erotic excesses, on the one hand, or his wordy, weighty preachifying, on the other.

Chanson pour elles

Ils me disent que tu es blonde
Et que toute blonde est perfide,
Même ils ajoutent "comme l'onde."
Je me ris de leur discours vide!
Tes yeux sont les plus beaux du monde
Et de ton sein je suis avide.

Ils me disent que tu es brune,
Qu'une brune a des yeux de braise
Et qu'un cœur qui cherche fortune
S'y brûle... Ô la bonne foutaise!
Ronde et fraîche comme la lune,
Vive ta gorge aux bouts de fraise!

Ils me disent de toi, châtaine:
Elle est fade, et rousse trop rose.
J'encague cette turlutaine,
Et de toi j'aime toute chose
De la chevelure, fontaine
D'ébène ou d'or (et dis, ô pose-
Les sur mon cœur), aux pieds de reine.

Song for the Ladies

They tell me you're a blonde; they say
That every blonde is wicked. Then
They add: "as sin." I laugh when they
Utter such rot, again, again…
Those eyes, those breasts: ah, how I pray
To make them ever mine, amen!

They tell me that you're brown-haired, you,
And that your eyes are fire, where might
Be badly burned hearts that pursue
Their fortune there… What blatherskite!
Round as the moon, and fresh: here's to
Your bosom's berry-tipped delight!

They talk about your chestnut hair,
Say it's a faded shade of red.
I tell them what to do with their
Damn tongues! From queenly toe to head—
Tresses of flowing gold, or rar-
Est jet!—I love you, there (come, spread
Them on my breast), and everywhere.

Fog!

Pour Mme ***

Ce brouillard de Paris est fade,
On dirait même qu'il est clair
Au prix de cette promenade
Que l'on appelle Leicester Square.

Mais le brouillard de Londres est
Savoureux comme non pas autres;
Je vous le dis, et fermes et
Pires les opinions nôtres!

Pourtant dans ce brouillard hagard
Ce qu'il faut retenir quand même
C'est, en dépit de tout hasard,
Que je l'adore et qu'elle m'aime.

Fog!

For Mme ***

Our Paris fog is dull; one might
Even say that, if you compare
Them, it could almost pass for bright
Next to the fog in Leicester Square.

The London fog is lush, not bland
Like other fogs; I'm telling you,
That's our unflagging judgment, and
We brook no other points of view.

Yet, in our sickish fog, the thing
To keep in mind unfailingly
Is that, whatever fate may bring,
I worship her, and she loves me.

Invectives (1896)

*L*ess than a year after Verlaine's death, Vanier published (in a nondescript order, mostly of his own choosing) the seventy-some social, political, personal, and even self-directed "invectives" that had yet to appear in print. Considering the material, it is hard not to believe that he did so more for his own benefit than for the greater glory of his poet-client-friend.

There seems to be little doubt that, had Verlaine himself had his say, and had he finally decided to bring out a collection that had been growing pell-mell during his last years, many, if not most, of the poems in this artificially constructed volume would not have been published. Remnants and rejects of other earlier collections, including the cannibalized *Cellulairement* and even the ultra-respectable *Sagesse,* a number of the disparate poems in *Invectives* had originally been earmarked for the ill-fated *Le Livre posthume,* only to be put aside thanks to the poet's better judgment; a better judgment apparently not shared, or at least not considered, by his longtime publisher.

Subject of acrimonious debate and dissension following its appearance, this second of Verlaine's posthumous collections, if it did succeed briefly in profiting Vanier, also tarnished for a time—fortunately also briefly—the reputation of its now defenseless creator. Bilious and cranky in spirit, contrived if not careless in form, often openly vulgar in language, the poems show little of Verlaine's gentility of expression or elegance of prosody. Nevertheless, a few of them do offer a certain saving grace in their humor, wry and acerbic though it is; and for that, if for nothing else, they deserve to be remembered.

※

Sonnet pour larmoyer

Juge de paix mieux qu'insolent
Et magistralement injuste,
Qui vas massif, ventre ballant,
Jambes cagneuses—et ce buste!

Je veux dire ton maltalent,
Ta manière rustique et fruste
D'être pédant… et somnolent,
Et sot, que de façon robuste!

Je n'ai pas oublié, non, non!
(Ce compliment de sorte neuve
Que je te rime en est la preuve.)

Je n'ai pas oublié ton nom,
Tes rengaines ni ta bedaine,
Ni ta dégaine—ni ma haine!

x x i

Sonnet to Weep Over

Magistrate more than insolent,
Inquisitor unjust (and more so),
Flaccid your belly, legs low-bent,
Massive your bulk—and oh that torso!

Manner much worse than impudent,
A boor you were; what's more, a bore, so
Pompous of speech, grandiloquent
(Except when dozing off, of course)! Oh

No, no, I don't forget—for shame!
(The proof: this honor that I do you,
Writing, new style, this sonnet to you.)

No, no, I don't forget your name,
Clichés that seemed to inundate you,
Your weight, your gait... or how I hate you!

X X I

Chanson pour boire

À Léon Vanier

Je suis un sale ivrogne, dam!
Et j'ai donc reçu d'Amsterdam
Un panier ou deux de Schiedam.

Mais seulement le péager
Qu'il me faut pourtant ménager
À moins que de le négliger

M'interdit—il a bien raison!—
D'introduire dans ma maison
Ce trop pardonnable poison.

Je vole à la gare du Nord,
Mais j'y pense: or voici que l'ord-
E misère est là qui me mord…

Hélas! comment faire, Vanier?
Je n'ai plus l'ombre d'un denier
Pour vous offrir un verre ou deux de ce panier.

L V

A Drink Song

For Léon Vanier

A drunken sot, that's what I am!
Just think; someone sent me a damn
Fine lot of gin—Schiedam—no sham!

From Amsterdam, a crate or two!
But for the customs, what to do?
The agent (I dare not pooh-pooh

Him!) won't release to me this berry
Brew—ah! the poison salutary!—
Without a sop pecuniary.

So off I scurry to the Gare
Du Nord; but there I find a jar-
Ring penury, my worst by far…

Alas, Vanier! Now, what say you?
Without the shadow of a sou
I can't go fetch a glass or two to treat you to.

L V

Autre chanson pour boire

À Léon Vanier

> Je triomphe et j'ai ce Schiedam
> (Qui ne me vient point d'Amsterdam
>   Mais de La Haye),
> Et j'en ai bu beaucoup, beaucoup,
> Trop peut-être et j'ai vu le loup
>   Sauter la haie.
>
> La haie, hélas! de ma raison,
> Sauter et fuir à l'horizon
>   Tel un cortège
> À lui tout seul, ce loup, de loups
> Et je dis: il me serait doux,
>   Puisque m'assiège
>
> Le remords—car c'est du remords,
> Et le remords c'est des rats morts
>   Dont l'odeur pue—
> De n'avoir encor partagé
> Ce Schiedam ô si fort que j'ai!
> Avec tel dont la note est due,
>
> —De partager (un peu) ce fier Schiedam que j'ai.

18 AVRIL 1893. / LVI

Another Drink Song

For Léon Vanier

When all is said and done, I win,
And get my crates of Schiedam gin
    (Sent to me not
From Amsterdam, but from The Hague, you
Know), and I gulp till, with the ague—
    Sot misbegot—

Trembling, I see a beast, pink-hued:
An elephant, just one—then two'd,
    Three'd, four'd… In fact,
A multitude—and think: "My, my,
What a swacked rotter (damn!) am I,"
    Compunction-racked

(But why? Remorse is like the plague sent
Down from on high): me and my Hague-sent
    Gin, that I still
Have failed to share—O brew divine,
Hearty Schiedam!—with colleague mine,
Party to my outstanding bill,

—Yes, share (a little of) this fine Schiedam divine!

18 APRIL 1893. / LVI

◁ 255 ▷

Rêve

Je renonce à la poésie!
Je vais être riche demain.
À d'autres je passe la main:
Qui veut, qui veut m'être un Sosie?

Bel emploi, j'en prends à témoin
Les bonnes heures de balade
Où, rimaillant quelque ballade,
Je passais mes nuits tard et loin.

Sous la lune lucide et claire
Les ponts luisaient insidieux,
L'eau baignait de flots gracieux
Paris gai comme un cimetière.

Je renonce à tout ce bonheur
Et je lègue aux jeunes ma lyre!
Enfants, héritez mon délire,
Moi j'hérite un sac suborneur.

L X V I

Dream

No! No more poetry! I'm through!
Tomorrow I'll be rich; so tell me,
I pass the deal: who wants to spell me?
Have I a Double? Who? Tell me, who?

Good job, solid career anon!
Witness my hours spent persevering,
Sauntering free and sonneteering,
Early and late, hither and yon.

The moon, that lucent luminary,
Lit up the bridges sinister;
Billows lapped Paris, cleansing her—
Paris, gay as a cemetery.

And so, seduced by wealth untold,
Thus do I yield the joys of rhyme,
For reason: for tomorrow I'm
Inheriting a sack of gold.

L X V I

Réveil

Je reviens à la poésie!
La richesse décidément
Ne veut pas de mon dénuement,
Et c'est un triste dénouement.

À moi la provende choisie,
L'eau claire et pure et ce pain sec
Quotidien non sans, avec,
Un gent petit air de rebec!

À moi le lit problématique
Aux nuits blanches, aux rêves noirs,
À moi les éternels espoirs
Pavanés des matins aux soirs!

À moi l'éthique et l'esthétique!
Je suis le poète fameux
Rimant des vers pharamineux
À l'ombre d'un quinquet fumeux!

Je suis l'âme par Dieu choisie
Pour charmer mes contemporains
Par tels rares et fins refrains
Chantés à jeun, ô cieux sereins!

Je reviens à la poésie.

LXVII

Awakening

It's back to poetry for me!
It's plain to see that wealth, largesse,
Care nothing for my neediness:
Sad cession to my dream's success!

Back to my daily grubbery:
Clear water and, in proper style,
A crust of bread, served up the while
With pleasant tune strummed on the viol!

Back to my bed, like some ascetic,
My somber dreams, my sleepless nights;
Back to my hopes, my fancy's flights,
A-strut from dawns to grim twilights!

Back to my ethic and aesthetic!
Again, the famous poet, I—
For better (or worse?) to versify—
Watching the wick glow, smoke, and die!

I am God's chosen soul, whom He
Selects to charm the age; but what
A chore, good heavens! to sing with but
An empty space to fill my gut!

It's back to poetry for me.

L X V I I

Posthumous

Mort!

Les Armes ont tu leurs ordres en attendant
De vibrer à nouveau dans des mains admirables
Ou scélérates, et, tristes, le bras pendant,
Nous allons, mal rêveurs, dans le vague des Fables.

Les Armes ont tu leurs ordres qu'on attendait
Même chez les rêveurs mensongers que nous sommes,
Honteux de notre bras qui pendait et tardait,
Et nous allons, désappointés, parmi les hommes.

Armes, vibrez! mains admirables, prenez-les,
Mains scélérates à défaut des admirables!
Prenez-les donc et faites signe aux En-allés
Dans les fables plus incertaines que les sables.

Tirez du rêve notre exode, voulez-vous?
Nous mourons d'être ainsi languides, presque infâmes!
Armes, parlez! Vos ordres vont être pour nous
La vie enfin fleurie au bout, s'il faut, des lames.

La mort que nous aimons, que nous eûmes toujours
Pour but de ce chemin où prospèrent la ronce
Et l'ortie, ô la mort sans plus ces émois lourds,
Délicieuse et dont la victoire est l'annonce!

DÉCEMBRE 1895.

Death

Our Swords' commands are silent now, expect
Much abler hands (or more perfidious)
To rattle in; and we—arms once erect—
Dreamers inept, sad, roam Worlds Fabulous.

Our Swords' commands are silent now, that one
Deemed fit by us—sham dreamers—to be used:
But we, ashamed of our limp arms, undone,
Wander the World of Men, baffled, bemused.

Rattle, you Swords! You, abler hands—you (or
Perfidious ones, for want of abler hands!),
Take them, and shake them at those Gone Before,
In fable-lands more fickle than the sands.

Wrench us free of the dream, our exodus,
Lest we die, languid, even slothfully!
Speak, Swords! Let your commands give birth, in us,
To life, at blade-points blooming, if need be.

O death! Dear to our hearts, death that was ever—
Though bramble-strewn the path—our destination;
Death, pleasing now: no pangs, no pains whatever;
Death that, in victory, sings its affirmation.

DECEMBER 1895.

‹ 263 ›

Epilogue

Quatrain

D'ailleurs en ce temps léthargique,
Sans gaîté comme sans remords,
Le seul rire encore logique,
C'est celui des têtes de morts.

Quatrain

With neither joy nor penitence
In these lethargic times, the one
And only laugh that still makes sense
Comes from a grinning skeleton.

Notes

Seascape (page 7)

> This very early poem, first appearing in the *Parnasse contemporain* of 1866, is typical of the intentionally impersonal descriptiveness that Verlaine was soon to abandon.

Night Scene (page 9)

> Besides the distinctly Baudelairean air of this poem, consistent with the young Verlaine's adulation of his celebrated predecessor, critics have pointed to a reminiscence of the equally admired Villon's "Ballade des pendus," and especially to the probable influence of Aloysius Bertrand's lugubriously romantic prose poem *Gaspard de la nuit.*

Sunsets (page 11)

> *line 13:* My use of "trolls" here was dictated not only by the music of the word but also by the fact that these legendary creatures traditionally have flaming red hair, not unlike Verlaine's *fantômes vermeils,* so appropriate in the context.

Autumn Song (page 17)

> *lines 7–8:* Despite the prohibition in English prosody against homophonic rhymes—a prohibition that does not exist in French—Verlaine's rhymes in this celebrated poem are so lush that I have chosen to violate the rule in an attempt to achieve even a little something of the same effect.

Woman and Cat (page 21)

> *line 6:* Although the French *mitaine* is today a half-glove, one that leaves the fingers exposed, in Verlaine's time it was also the equivalent of our "mitten," which seems to be the intended meaning here.

Nevermore (page 25)

> The *Poèmes saturniens* contain two poems entitled "Nevermore," of which this is the second, and both of which, by obviously invoking Poe's celebrated "The Raven," indirectly bespeak Verlaine's admiration for Baudelaire, for whom Poe was a literary idol.

Moonlight (page 29)

line 2: Critics have called attention to Verlaine's somewhat punning metonymic use of *bergamasques* to indicate people rather than their music, derived from the Italian town of Bergamo. Le Dantec, in his critical edition, notes that Shakespeare had done likewise in *A Midsummer Night's Dream*. See Paul Verlaine, *Œuvres poétiques complètes*, ed. Yves-Gérard Le Dantec, rev. ed. Jacques Borel (Paris: Gallimard, 1962; reprinted 1968), p. 1087 (hereinafter cited as *OPC;* page citations are to the reprint).

Pantomime (page 31)

The characters here portrayed are, of course, from the stock personnel of the Italian *commedia dell'arte*, as filtered through Verlaine's admiration of the eighteenth-century painter of fantasy scenes, Watteau. Pierrot and Arlequin, the Gallic successors of the *zanni* Pedrolino and Arlecchino, would develop in their own right as characters in the French pantomimic and theatrical canon.

On the Grass (page 33)

As has often been suggested, this poem was probably inspired by Watteau's fantasy *L'Île enchantée*. The eighteenth-century flavor is made all the more evident by the reference to (La) Camargo, a famous dancer whose real name was Marie-Anne Cuppi (1710–1770), and who was immortalized on canvas by the painter Nicolas Lancret.

The Lane (page 35)

Although composed of fourteen lines, this early poem is in no formal sense a sonnet, a form in which the young Verlaine had already written and in which the mature poet would continue to do with some frequency and variety. I have preserved in my translation the capricious rhyme scheme of the original.

Innocents We (page 39)

line 11: I have accepted the Le Dantec-Borel edition's reading of *spécieux* (false) as opposed to variants indicated: *spéciaux* (special) and *précieux* (precious). (See *OPC*, p. 1088.)

Seashells (page 43)

line 13: Victor Hugo particularly admired Verlaine's last line, whose allusion is perhaps less veiled than it might first appear if we consider that the young poet was, at this early period, writing a number of blatantly erotic verses to which the general public was not usually privy, and would do so off and on throughout his career.

Puppets (page 45)

I have taken a few minor liberties in this poem of *commedia dell'arte* inspiration, since Verlaine himself seems a little confused about his characters. The two buffoons, Scaramouche and Pulcinella, are clear enough, but the reference to *l'excellent docteur bolonais* is much less so, considering that the *dottore* of the Italian company was neither a medical doctor nor, as suggested here, an herbalist. I have opted for the suggestion that it was Pantaleone, the stock old man, who was intended, since it was he who had the winsome daughter (Colombine). As for the Spanish pirate referred to, Verlaine appears to have turned the traditional "braggart warrior" inherited from the Roman theater into a buccaneer, and I do likewise.

Mandolin (page 51)

In addition to the stock character Clitander of the Italian *commedia*, Verlaine here peoples his stylized scenario with three others borrowed from the traditional pastoral romances: Tircis, Aminta—whose namesake was immortalized by Tasso—and Damis.

For Clymène (page 53)

At the risk of stating the obvious, I call the reader's attention to the phenomenon of synesthesia—the simultaneous relationship of the several senses—that dominates this early poem and that was to characterize much Symbolist poetry.

Love Cast Down (page 59)

This poem, with its symbolic disintegration of Love, and the following one, with its atmosphere of muted despair, are clearly intended by Verlaine as foreshadowings of the end of this collection's "Gallant Revels," nostalgically remembered by the spectral lovers of "Colloque sentimental" (see p. 62).

"Morning star, before you pale…" (page 67)
The reader will notice here Verlaine's formal tour de force: the composition of two poems in one, each presenting a unified whole but meshing with the other in perfectly logical fashion.

"Among the trees…" (page 69)
Among the many Verlaine poems set to music by famous and not-so-famous composers, this one and the next, in settings by Fauré, are among the best known and most widely performed.

"A Saint set in her stained-glass glow…" (page 71)
line 16: The allusion, clearly, is to the Germanic origin of the given name of Verlaine's fiancée, Mathilde Mauté.

"It's the languorous ecstasy…" (page 77)
First of the *Romances sans paroles,* and originally published in May of 1872, this *ariette oubliée* (forgotten air) was inspired, as indicated in the epigraph, by a well-known air in *Ninette à la cour,* a two-act comedy by popular eighteenth-century dramatist Charles-Simon Favart, apparently called to Verlaine's attention by Rimbaud. (See Le Dantec-Borel, *OPC,* pp. 1100–1101.)

"Like city's rain, my heart…" (page 79)
The epigraph attributed to Rimbaud has never been found in his works and is presumed to be lost.

"Bright in the evening's gray and pinkish blur…" (page 81)
Verlaine takes as his epigraph the opening line of "Doléance," a poem in the collection *Rhapsodies,* published in 1832 by Pétrus Borel, influential Romantic poet and novelist.
line 6: The "Elle" referred to is no doubt Verlaine's estranged wife Mathilde, and the setting, their apartment on Rue Nicolet in Paris, to which her family obstinately barred his entrance after their separation.

It is assumed that the poem was written in the early months of 1872, before the couple's brief reconciliation.

line 12: Since it is impossible to know if Verlaine intended the disparity in rhyme between the first sestet (*ababba*) and the second (*abaaba*), I remain faithful to the ambiguity by choosing a similar, though not identical, disparity.

"Reflections in the fogbound rivulet..." (page 89)

The epigraph is taken from "Sur l'ombre que faisoient des arbres dans l'eau," the seventh of the *Lettres diverses* of the seventeenth-century freethinker and man of letters Cyrano de Bergerac, immortalized in Edmond Rostand's celebrated play bearing his name.

Walcourt (page 91)

This poem is one of a group inspired by Verlaine's impressions of Belgium— *Paysages belges*—during the early days of his escapade there with Rimbaud. His allusion to the tale of the Wandering Jew is of interest in that the legend had flourished in Flanders for many centuries, and the last supposed appearance of the mythical character, known by the name of Isaac Laquedem, had occurred in Brussels as late as 1774.

Charleroi (page 93)

The Kobolds, in Germanic—and particularly Flemish—folklore, were a race of goblins or night spirits, said especially to frequent mines. Verlaine's allusion to them in his terse and none-too-flattering evocation of Charleroi is appropriate, given the Belgian town's heavy mining and metal industries.

"Above the roof the sky is fair..." (page 111)

My remarks about the usefulness of biographical detail (pp. xv–xvi) are especially pertinent here. Unless one realizes that this poem was composed in a prison cell, through whose window the poet views a small corner of the outside world, it is reduced to an exercise in the expression of general angst rather than of a very specific despair.

"The horn's sound in the wood sobs dolefully..." (page 113)

Written early in 1873, before Verlaine's prison stay and alleged conversion, this poem, much closer in inspiration to his earlier works than to those of *Sagesse*, is probably the first, chronologically, of that collection. (See Le Dantec-Borel, *OPC*, p. 1132.)

"The wind whips through the bushes, green…" (page 115)
The original of this poem, dating from Verlaine's pre-prison travels with Rimbaud in 1873, contained only the first fourteen lines and was to be included in the collection *Cellulairement*. When it was eventually incorporated into *Sagesse*, Verlaine added the last six lines to give the poem a spiritual touch ostensibly in keeping with his prison conversion.

"The hedges billow like the sea's…" (page 117)
Though there is some doubt as to the dating of this poem from *Sagesse*, Verlaine's annotation ("Stickney, 75") confirms at least that it was inspired by one of his stays in England—in Lincolnshire, to be exact—where he spent a year teaching French upon his release from prison.

" 'The city!' Gaudy cluster of white stones…" (page 119)
The Le Dantec-Borel edition notes that the indicated date of this poem, "Paris, 77," is contradicted in another manuscript where the date given is March 1876.
line 9: Often capitalized, the common noun *la thébaïde*—from Thebae, a city in northern Egypt where early Christian ascetics would go for meditation and contemplation—refers, in literary language, to a place of utter solitude and retreat.
line 12: The above-mentioned manuscript gives Verlaine's own explication of this last line as referring to his estranged wife and son, double source of his angst.

Pierrot (page 123)
Léon Valade, to whom this poem is dedicated, was a Parnassian contemporary of Verlaine's, known mainly for his tableaux of Parisian life and a number of satirical poems.
line 1: The *vieil air* is, of course, the well-known folk tune "Mon ami Pierrot." But Verlaine's reference to it is curious in that, in the song, it is the neighbor, not Pierrot himself—he of the traditional white costume and

mime's powdered face—who complains that his candle is "dead" (*"Ma chandelle est morte, je n'ai plus de feu...."* [My candle is dead, I have no more fire....]).

The Skeleton (page 125)

Albert Mérat was author of several sonnet collections and one of the poets with whom Verlaine fraternized early in his career, somewhat on the fringes of the Parnassian movement. Critics have called attention to traces of Mérat's realism in some of Verlaine's youthful works, though the present poem, dating from 1869, smacks also to some extent of the much admired Baudelaire, humor aside.

line 7: The reference in the original to *nos capitaines Fracasse* (which I omit in translation for lack of familiarity) alludes to the blustering hero of Théophile Gautier's popular historical fantasy *Le Capitaine Fracasse,* probably written as early as 1836 but not published until 1863.

Ars Poetica (page 127)

There is a certain irony in Verlaine's dedication of this famous poem to Charles Morice, influential poet and theoretician of Symbolism.

Though his *La Littérature de tout à l'heure* (1889) calls for the same suggestivity and impressionistic vagueness that Verlaine champions here, when the poem first appeared in the review *Paris-Moderne* in November 1882 (though dated April 1874, and intended for the collection *Cellulairement,* whose poems of prison inspiration were later included elsewhere), Morice's review, under the penname Karl Mohr, was quite negative. Nevertheless, Morice was eventually to become one of Verlaine's staunchest admirers and friends.

lines 25–28: Verlaine's harsh indictment of rhyme is more than curious considering his own obvious devotion to, and mastery of, its effects throughout his poetic career.

Allegory (page 131)

Jules-Emmanuel Valadon was a popular painter of the period, known especially for his landscapes, still lifes, and portraits, whose representational style Verlaine seems to be imitating in this sonnet of apparently Parnassian inspiration. The poem, dating from 1868 and dedicated to him, is thought, in fact, to have been inspired by one of his canvases.

Circumspection (page 133)

Originally published in 1867, this sonnet, when incorporated into *Jadis et naguère* as one of the "yesteryear" poems, acquired its dedication to Gaston Sénéchal, a poet little known in Verlaine's time and quite forgotten in our own. Without evidence to the contrary, I believe that Verlaine chose this way to thank him for a sonnet, "Moyen-Âge," that Sénéchal had dedicated to him in the short-lived but influential review *La Nouvelle Rive Gauche* (February 2–9, 1883), a year before the publication of *Jadis et naguère*. The sonnet in question, in obvious homage, echoes the style for which Verlaine had already become celebrated.

line 14: Verlaine was obviously bucking tradition by making Nature male rather than female (even if one were to accept a curious variant of the line, namely: "La nature, ce *chien* féroce et taciturne"). Perhaps he did so because of metrical demands, the one-syllable *dieu* (god) fitting where the three-syllable *déesse* (goddess) would not, at least if he wanted to preserve the rest of the line as is. Be that as it may, I follow him in his very untraditional—and un-romantic—personification.

Languor (page 135)

The dedication to the popular comic dramatist Georges Courteline (pseudonym of Georges Moineaux) perhaps underscores the probable satiric intent of this well-known sonnet. Originally published in 1883, it was quickly seized upon as an *art poétique* by the adepts of the so-called *Décadent* movement, a kind of exaggerated Symbolism that flourished in the late 1880s and that adopted Verlaine, willy-nilly, as its artistic conscience.

line 10: Verlaine gives the name *Bathylle* to the companion (or perhaps the slave?) of the poem's voice probably in recollection of the decadent ephebe Bathyllus of the Anacreontic poems, or—less likely, I think—Bathyllus of Alexandria, a comic dancer of the first century B.C.

Prologue (page 137)

Probably dating from January 1883 (see Le Dantec-Borel, *OPC*, p. 1161), these introductory quatrains serve as the prologue to the *Naguère* section of the *Jadis et naguère* collection.

"Your voice was deep and low…" (page 141)

Composed during one of Verlaine's several hospital stays, this poem, dated December 1887, was inspired by Verlaine's deep affection for his former student Lucien Létinois, who had died a few years earlier.

For Georges Verlaine (page 145)

Although a substantial portion of the collection *Amour* deals with Verlaine's affection for, and mourning of, his student Lucien Létinois, the volume, with its melange of quasi-religious, occasionally political, and personal inspirations, was, in fact, dedicated *in toto* to his son. The present poem, last of the collection, was dated May 1887, hence composed shortly before the volume's publication the following year.

Spring (page 151)

This sonnet and the one following, along with four others of equally evident Sapphic content, all grouped under the title *Les Amies*, date from Verlaine's youth. Of clearly Baudelairean inspiration, the poems were eventually revised and incorporated into the collection *Parallèlement*. They were, it should be noted, not Verlaine's only incursion into both the hetero- and homoerotic, the best-known example of which is his collaboration with Rimbaud, the "Sonnet sur le trou du cul" (Sonnet on the Asshole).

lines 1–8: I have followed the young Verlaine's unorthodox change of rhyme scheme between quatrains, whether the result of his negligence or his intent.

False Impression (page 159)

Dated July 11, 1873, the day of his imprisonment in Brussels after the Rimbaud affair, this poem was originally intended (minus the third stanza, which was subsequently added) to be included in the collection *Cellulairement.*

Other (page 163)

line 1: The opening line of this prison poem, dating from 1873, presents a pun on the two meanings of *souci* ("marigold" and "care, woe"). That

Verlaine did, indeed, have both flowers and woes in mind, in his tableau of the yard at the Petits-Carmes prison, is indicated by a passage from his confessional *Mes Prisons*, quoted in Le Dantec-Borel (*OPC*, p. 1207), in which he describes the little garden "tout en la fleur jaune nommée souci" (planted with the yellow flower called marigold) outside his cell.

Tantalized (page 167)

As the subject makes clear, this poem, composed at the prison in Mons, Belgium, to which Verlaine had been transferred at the end of August 1874, was originally to figure in *Cellulairement*, and dates, with a few variants, from no later than early September of that year.

line 5: one of the variants mentioned—the reading of *cieux* (skies) for *dieux* (gods), indicated in Le Dantec-Borel (*OPC*, p. 1208), but uncommented on—seems rather unlikely in the context.

The Last Stanza (page 169)

line 5: The allusion to "les roseaux bavards d'un monde vain" seems like an echo—if only unconscious on the part of the newly devout Verlaine—of Pascal's celebrated definition of Man as "un roseau pensant" (a thinking reed).

In the Style of Paul Verlaine (page 171)

Verlaine's cynical yet nostalgic evocation of his early style—obvious in his very unveiled references to the *Fêtes galantes, Poèmes saturniens,* and *Romances sans paroles*—probably dates from May 1885 and is typical of the self-parodying element common to much of his verse from around that period.

Limbo (page 173)

First appearing in the July 19–23, 1885, number of Léo Trézenik's journal *Lutèce*, successor to *La Nouvelle Rive Gauche*, this poem bore the dedication "À P. V.," i.e., "To P(aul) V(erlaine)." (See Le Dantec-Borel, *OPC*, p. 1211.) If the subject is reasonably clear—Verlaine's recognition of the combat within himself of reason and imagination, with the unenviable victory of the latter—the title, nevertheless, remains a little obscure. I tend to suspect that, since it was originally published along with "Lombes" (see p. 176), the apparent French wordplay was at least a consideration.

line 31: Verlaine supplied a note in the *Lutèce* publication explaining that the venerable literary metaphor describing imagination as *la folle du logis* (the madwoman of the house) originated with Saint Theresa. (See Le Dantec-Borel, *OPC*, p. 1211.)

The Last "Fête Galante" (page 179)

The Le Dantec-Borel edition (*OPC*, p. 1211) rejects the hypothesis that this poem, all but the third quatrain of which was first published (with "Limbes" and "Lombes") in July 1885, had actually been written earlier, intended for the collection *Fêtes galantes* but omitted by the squeamish publisher because of its clear homosexual overtones, rather than as a self-parodic, over-the-shoulder glance some fifteen years later.

line 16: The *embarquement pour Sodome et Gomorrhe* is an evident sarcastic thrust at the stylized pastoral fantasies of the *Fêtes galantes,* summed up in the prototypical painting of Watteau, *L'Embarquement pour Cythère.*

Recollection of Manchester (page 183)

These couplets, one of the many poems added to the second edition, commemorate a lecture that Verlaine gave in Manchester on December 1, 1893, on the subject of Racine and Shakespeare. The Le Dantec-Borel edition (*OPC*, p. 1243) notes that Theodore C. London, to whom they were dedicated, was a young local clergyman who gave Verlaine an especially warm welcome.

line 1: The borough of Salford, as the verse implies, is a stone's throw from Manchester, just across the river Irwell.

lines 13–14: If Verlaine is saying, as I understand him, that the Manchester "elite" were naïve enough to think he was the author of verses quoted from Racine's tragedy *Esther,* one might suspect the authenticity of the anecdote, fabricated, perhaps, to take advantage of a very convenient rhyme.

For Edmond Lepelletier (page 185)

Lepelletier, a long-time close friend of Verlaine, was the author of the first important study of his life and works: *Paul Verlaine, sa vie, son œuvre* (Paris: Mercure de France, 1907).

For Arthur Rimbaud (page 187)
Originally presenting a number of variants, this poem was first published in August 1889, two years before Rimbaud's death.

line 1: The Le Dantec-Borel edition (*OPC*, p. 1244) cites the explanation, by Henri Mondor, of Verlaine's emphatically capitalized *ET*, as echoing (and slightly altering) the poet Lamartine's description of Lord Byron as *mortel, ange, ou* (i.e., "or") *démon.*

For Bibi-Purée (page 189)
The colorful Bibi-Purée (or Bibi-la-Purée) was a well-known denizen of the Quartier Latin: a curious Bohemian whose real name is thought to have been André-Joseph Salis and who virtually worshiped Verlaine, serving him both as errand-boy and—it is supposed—as occasional sexual partner. (See Le Dantec-Borel, *OPC*, pp. 1249.)

"Yes, despite your cruel excess…" (page 199)
It is believed that, like the rest of the *Chansons pour Elle*, written during and between hospital stays for a variety of ailments and published in 1891, this one was inspired by Verlaine's liaison with the less-than-sophisticated Eugénie Krantz. The earthy, often banal nature of the volume, quite at odds with the religious fervor of the triptych *Sagesse-Amour-Bonheur*, is generally taken to prove the point. My version attempts to reproduce the rhyming liberties typical of the late Verlaine, all the more striking in this collection after the more traditional, regular rhymes of the preceding religious verse.

"True, we don't know when to quit…" (page 205)
My admittedly rather free rendition attempts to reproduce both the erotic sense and the popular, almost cabaret-like sound of Verlaine's original; the latter, by duplicating his alternating seven- and two-syllable lines, and by using near-rhymes to suggest his own rhyming liberties. (The reader should note that in French versification words ending in mute *e* are not proper rhymes for those that do not, similar sound notwithstanding. Therefore, such combinations as *"esprit / chérie," "corps / encore,"* etc. do not really rhyme, any more than do my "quit / sweet," "chin / again," etc.)

"Blonde? Brown? Which is your hair?..." (page 207)

line 7: Verlaine's seven-syllable line ("Est-il sensible ou moqueur,"), among the analogous preceding and succeeding five-syllable lines, would seem to be an oversight, and I have chosen not to follow him in it.

"I dreamed of you last night; and you..." (page 213)

line 13: Exceptionally and inexplicably, Verlaine offers no rhyme for this line. Without presuming to second-guess him, I provide one in my version, extending a single rhyme over the last three lines, an expedient he himself uses elsewhere. (See, for example, "Tu crois au marc de café...," p. 208.)

"You've often been unkind..." (page 221)

Like all the poems in *Odes en son honneur,* this one, with its down-to-earth language and erratic rhymes, was probably inspired by Philomène Boudin. I have taken the liberty of restoring, typographically, the metric differences between stanzas 1, 4 and 2, 3, contrary to Verlaine's own (or Le Dantec's) presentation (*OPC,* pp. 770–71).

Last Hope (page 231)

There is evidence that this sonnet was originally arranged as follows: quatrain, tercet, quatrain, tercet. (See Le Dantec-Borel, *OPC,* p. 1289.) This would help account for Verlaine's curious rhyme scheme (which I have kept), producing a pattern of *abba / ccd / effe / dgg,* which, while not exactly orthodox, is at least less bizarre than the one produced by the present disposition of the lines.

"It's thanks to you I see how I..." (page 237)

Verlaine had met the young artist F.-A. Cazals in the spring of 1886, and maintained with him over the ensuing years an often tempestuous friendship, colored by the poet's frequent jealousies and rejected sentimental advances. Nevertheless, Cazals remained a solicitous friend, especially during Verlaine's most trying times. The Le Dantec-Borel edition (*OPC,* p. 1300) notes that his celebrated sketch, showing the silhouetted Verlaine leaning on his cane, served as the frontispiece to the original edition of *Épigrammes* in 1894.

Accompanying a Sketch (The Siege of Paris) (page 239)

The Le Dantec-Borel edition (*OPC*, p. 1301) notes that this epigraph, eventually included in *Épigrammes*, is a revised version of a quatrain dated October 29, 1870, during the siege of Paris, and originally accompanying an unflattering sketch in Régamey's volume *Verlaine dessinateur* (Paris: Floury, 1896). It represents the poet in a broad-lapeled greatcoat, heavily bearded, sitting slumped at a table in the Café du Gaz, on the Rue de Rivoli.

On a Copy of Les Fleurs du mal (page 241)

Originally appearing in the quixotic (and often erotic) *Album zutique* of 1871—collaborative effort of a number of young artistic dissidents of the period—this quatrain was later included in *Épigrammes*. (See Le Dantec-Borel, *OPC*, p. 163.)

Song for the Ladies (page 245)

lines 17–19: This poem, with its extra final line, is typical of the late Verlaine's cavalier formal liberties (or, perhaps, inadvertences). As for my own liberty in splitting the word "rarest" over the line, while he splits only a hyphenated phrase (*pose-les*), the somewhat frivolous practice is not uncommon in his work of this period. (See, for example, "A Drink Song," p. 253, lines 11–12.)

Fog! (page 247)

Most of the poems in this, the first of Verlaine's posthumously published collections, were written between 1893 and 1895, and are thought to have been inspired by his latter-day muses Eugénie and Philomène, as well as others, among them no doubt the enigmatic "Mme ***" of this poem's dedication.

Sonnet to Weep Over (page 251)

It is hypothesized that the object of Verlaine's bitter but humorous invective—ironically left anonymous—was one of those magistrates involved in his early marital difficulties. (See Le Dantec-Borel, *OPC*, p. 1310.) Formally, although his own rhymes here are quite orthodox throughout, I have taken the liberty of treating them in translation with the capriciousness one finds in much of his verse of this late period.

A Drink Song (page 253)

Verlaine's title is, I think, intentionally askew: not a *chanson à boire*, a "drinking song" (that is, to be sung while drinking), but a *chanson pour boire* (that is, for the purpose of drinking). Léon Vanier, to whom the *chanson* is dedicated, was Verlaine's longtime friend—despite a variety of squabbles and one serious falling-out—and publisher of many of his collections, among them *Invectives*.

line 3: Schiedam, a small town near Rotterdam, was known for its gin. Verlaine no doubt came to appreciate it during his lecture tour in November 1892 in The Hague, Leyden, and Amsterdam.

lines 11–12: Regarding Verlaine's (and my) word-splitting, see "Song for the Ladies," p. 282, note.

Another Drink Song (page 255)

The reader will appreciate that, while my version of this sequel to the preceding follows the form and content of the original French, and respects its spirit(s), I have had to make rather free with detail.

Awakening (page 259)

The "invective" element of this poem and of the tongue-in-cheek preceding one, both first published November 1, 1896, was apparently not directed, like most in the collection, at someone in particular, but rather at circumstances in general.

Death (page 263)

With the possible exception of a rather trifling poem intended for the collection *Biblio-Sonnets* (commissioned by a Parisian bookseller and eventually published, incomplete, in 1913), this is thought to be the last poem Verlaine ever wrote. The development of its theme—the poet's rejection of the world of dream that had animated much of his poetry—is studied by Octave Nadal in a lengthy passage quoted in Le Dantec-Borel (*OPC,* pp. 1357–59).

Quatrain (page 267)

Part of no collection during Verlaine's lifetime, this quatrain, with its Baudelairean conceit, was written as an epigraph to Villiers de l'Isle-Adam's novel *Claire Lenoir* (1867), and appears as such in chapter 4.

(See Le Dantec-Borel, *OPC*, p. 1091.) Though it dates from early in his career, before the many real misfortunes and torments he was to suffer throughout his life, I have chosen to place it here, at the end of my presentation, as an apt conclusion, symbolically closing the circle.

Acknowledgments

The following translations in this collection have previously been published and are reprinted here with permission:

"Night Scene," "Cortège," and "Ars Poetica" in *The Formalist* 9, no. 2 (fall/winter 1998); and "Allegory" (page 131 in this volume) and "Circumspection" in *Partisan Review* 66, no. 2 (spring 1999).

Index of Titles and First lines